# IT SERVICE MANAGE

## BCS, THE CHARTERED INSTITUTE FOR IT

BCS, The Chartered Institute for IT champions the global IT profession and the interests of individuals engaged in that profession for the benefit of all. We promote wider social and economic progress through the advancement of information technology, science and practice. We bring together industry, academics, practitioners and government to share knowledge, promote new thinking, inform the design of new curricula, shape public policy and inform the public.

Our vision is to be a world-class organisation for IT. Our 70,000 strong membership includes practitioners, businesses, academics and students in the UK and internationally. We deliver a range of professional development tools for practitioners and employees. A leading IT qualification body, we offer a range of widely recognised qualifications.

**Further Information**
BCS, The Chartered Institute for IT,
First Floor, Block D,
North Star House, North Star Avenue,
Swindon, SN2 1FA, United Kingdom.
T +44 (0) 1793 417 424
F +44 (0) 1793 417 444
**www.bcs.org/contact**

**http://shop.bcs.org/**

# IT SERVICE MANAGEMENT
Support for your ITSM
Foundation exam
Third edition

**Ernest Brewster, Richard Griffiths, Aidan Lawes,
John Sansbury**

Published by BCS Learning & Development Ltd, a wholly owned subsidiary of BCS, The Chartered Institute for IT, First Floor, Block D, North Star House, North Star Avenue, Swindon, SN2 1FA, United Kingdom.
www.bcs.org

ISBN: 978-1-78017-318-4
PDF ISBN: 978-1-78017-319-1
ePUB ISBN: 978-1-78017-320-7
Kindle ISBN: 978-1-78017-321-4

Ebook available

British Cataloguing in Publication Data.
A CIP catalogue record for this book is available at the British Library.

Disclaimer:
The views expressed in this book are of the author(s) and do not necessarily reflect the views of BCS Learning & Development Ltd except where explicitly stated as such.

Although every care has been taken by the authors and BCS Learning & Development Ltd in the preparation of the publication, no warranty is given by the authors or BCS Learning & Development Ltd as publisher as to the accuracy or completeness of the information contained within it and neither the authors nor BCS Learning & Development Ltd shall be responsible or liable for any loss or damage whatsoever arising by virtue of such information or any instructions or advice contained within this publication or by any of the aforementioned.

BCS books are available at special quantity discounts to use as premiums and sales promotions, or for use in corporate training programmes. Please visit out Contact Use page at www.bcs.org/contact

Typeset by Lapiz Digital Services, Chennai, India.
Printed at Hobbs the Printers Ltd, Hampshire, UK.

# CONTENTS

# LIST OF FIGURES AND TABLES

# AUTHORS

**Ernest Brewster** has over 30 years' experience in IT, including 20 years as a senior manager in various public sector organisations, latterly as Head of IT at Fife Council, one of Scotland's largest local authorities with over 15,000 personal computers and a network linking several hundred separate sites. He is a long-time champion of ITIL® service management, with a record of implementing ITIL-based good practice in complex organisations, and an expert in strategy development, programme and project management, business process re-engineering and public procurement. Ernest is an ex-member of SOCITM's National Executive Committee and a contributor to several of SOCITM's MAPIT (now Insight) publications.

**Richard Griffiths** is an experienced and respected service management expert, and has worked as practitioner, trainer and consultant in all aspects of ITIL for a number of organisations worldwide. He has been a question compiler and examiner at all levels for ten years and uses the knowledge gained from running many Foundation courses to tailor his writing to the audience of potential candidates.

**Aidan Lawes** is one the world's leading independent authorities on, and a passionate champion of, IT service management (ITSM). Educated in New Zealand, he started his working life there in the insurance industry, before leaving to travel. On settling in the UK, he joined the Civil Service and entered the world of IT. There followed 20 years working for ICL in a variety of training and consultancy roles around the globe, including working on major service management projects in the financial and public sectors in Europe. From 1999 to 2007, he was CEO of *it*SMF UK and International, overseeing phenomenal membership and revenue growth, and spreading the SM gospel globally. Aidan is a Fellow of both the ISM and BCS, and has contributed to many ITSM publications (including ITIL), co-authored the BSI standard and its International successor (ISO/IEC 20000), chaired the ITIL V3 refresh programme board and participates in many initiatives to raise professional standards. In his spare time, Aidan is a passionate rugby fan, supporting the All Blacks and anyone playing against Australia.

**John Sansbury** been a service management practitioner for 35 years, a consultant for 20 years, a service management examiner since 1996 and a trainer for seven years. He has been helping organisations deliver real business value from IT. As a practitioner, he learnt his trade with Philips and London Electricity (now EDF) where he helped introduce capacity management (the interesting bit where you meet business representatives to understand their plans, not the techie, modelling stuff), negotiated the SLAs with the business and developed one of the world's first business-unit based charge-back systems. As a consultant and Global Head of Practice for Service Management, he has worked with organisations across the world to analyse and improve their

IT performance and service management processes and deliver increased stakeholder value. John is a Chartered Fellow of BCS, the Founder of the Classic Corvette Club UK, a husband of 33 years and the proud father of two successful sons. He has also written the guide to the OSA Intermediate Capability exam and is currently drafting the guide to the role of the Service Level Manager. Together with a colleague, John has also written the ITIL process maturity self-assessment model for Axelos.

# ABBREVIATIONS

| | |
|---|---|
| **BCM** | Business continuity management |
| **BIA** | Business impact analysis |
| **BRM** | Business relationship management |
| **CAB** | Change advisory board |
| **CI** | Configuration item |
| **CMDB** | Configuration management database |
| **CMIS** | Capacity management information system |
| **CMMI** | Capability Maturity Model Integration |
| **CMS** | Configuration management system |
| **COBIT** | Control OBjectives for Information and related Technology |
| **CRM** | Customer relationship management |
| **CSF** | Critical success factor |
| **CSI** | Continual service improvement |
| **DIKW** | Data-to-Information-to-Knowledge-to-Wisdom |
| **DML** | Definitive media library |
| **ECAB** | Emergency change advisory board |
| **EFQM** | The European Foundation for Quality Management |
| **eSCM–SP** | eSourcing Capability Model for Service Providers |
| **ISM** | Information security management |
| **ISMS** | Information security management system |
| **ISO** | International Organization for Standardization |
| **ITSCM** | IT service continuity management |
| **ITSM** | IT service management |
| **itSMF** | IT Service Management Forum |
| **KPI** | Key performance indicator |

| | |
|---|---|
| **MTBF** | Mean time between failures |
| **MTBSI** | Mean time between service incidents |
| **MTRS** | Mean time to restore service |
| **OLA** | Operational level agreement |
| **PBA** | Pattern of business activity |
| **RACI** | An example of an authority matrix: responsible, accountable, consulted, informed |
| **RFC** | Request for change |
| **ROI** | Return on investment |
| **SAC** | Service acceptance criterion |
| **SACM** | Service asset and configuration management |
| **SCD** | Supplier and contracts database |
| **SD** | Service design |
| **SDP** | Service design package |
| **SIP** | Service improvement plan (or programme) |
| **SKMS** | Service knowledge management system |
| **SLA** | Service level agreement |
| **SLAM** | SLA monitoring |
| **SLM** | Service level management |
| **SLR** | Service level requirements |
| **SM** | Service management |
| **SO** | Service operation/Service option |
| **SOX** | Sarbanes–Oxley |
| **SPM** | Service portfolio management |
| **SS** | Service strategy |
| **ST** | Service transition |
| **TCO** | Total cost of ownership |
| **TSO** | The Stationery Office |
| **UC** | Underpinning contract |
| **VBF** | Vital business function |
| **VOI** | Value on investment |

# GLOSSARY

**Capabilities**   The ability of an organisation, person, process, application, configuration item or IT service to carry out an activity. Capabilities are intangible assets of an organisation.

**Customer**   Someone who buys goods or services. The customer of an IT service provider is the person or group who defines and agrees the service level targets. The term is also sometimes used informally to mean user.

**Function**   A self-contained unit of an organisation that carries out one or more processes or activities (e.g. the service desk or IT operations).

**Operational level agreement**   An operational level agreement (OLA) is an agreement between two teams or functions within an IT service provider. It supports the IT service provider's delivery of IT services to the customers and the service levels contained in the corresponding SLA. The OLA defines the items or services to be provided and the responsibilities of each party.

**Process**   A process is a set of activities and procedures intended to achieve a specific objective. A process may include any of the roles, responsibilities, tools and management controls required to meet the objectives reliably. A process may define policies, standards, guidelines, activities and work instructions if they are needed.

**Resource**   A generic term that includes IT infrastructure, people, money or anything else that might help to deliver an IT service. Resources are considered to be assets of an organisation.

**Risk**   An event that could cause damage or loss, or affect the ability to meet objectives. Risk can also be defined as the uncertainty of outcome. A risk is measured by the probability of the event, the vulnerability of the asset to that event and the impact it would have if it occurred.

**Role**   A set of responsibilities, activities and authorities assigned to a person or team. A role is defined in a process or function. One person or team may have multiple roles (e.g. the roles of configuration manager and change manager may be carried out by a single person).

**Service**   A service is essentially a means of delivering value to customers. This is done by facilitating outcomes that customers want to achieve without the ownership of specific costs and risks.

**Service design package**   The document(s) defining all relevant aspects of an IT service together with their requirements through each stage of the service's lifecycle. A service design package is usually produced each time a new IT service is introduced, for major changes to an IT service or for an IT service retirement.

**Service improvement plan (or programme) (SIP)**   A formal plan to introduce improvements to a process or IT service.

**Service level agreement**   A service level agreement (SLA) is an agreement between an IT service provider and a customer that describes the IT service and service levels, and specifies the responsibilities of both parties.

**Service management**   Service management is a set of specialised organisational capabilities for providing value to customers in the form of services.

**Service package**   A service package comprises two or more services combined to offer a solution to a specific type of customer requirement or to support specific business outcomes. A service package can include a combination of core services, enabling services and enhancing services, and provides specific levels of utility and warranty.

**Strategic asset**   Strategic assets are assets that provide the basis for core competence, distinctive performance, durable advantage and qualifications to participate in business opportunities. IT organisations can use the guidance provided by ITIL to transform their service management capabilities into strategic assets.

**Supplier**   A third party responsible for supplying goods or services.

**User**   A person who uses the IT service on a day-to-day basis. Users are distinct from customers because some customers do not use the IT services directly.

**Utility**   Functionality offered by a product or service to meet a particular need. Utility is often summarised as 'what it does'.

**Vital business function**   A vital business function is that element of a business process critical to the success of the business.

**Warranty**   A promise or guarantee that a product or service will meet its agreed requirements.

# USEFUL WEBSITES

**www.efqm.org**
European Foundation for Quality Management

**www.isaca.org**
Information Systems Audit and Control Association

**www.iso.org**
International Organization for Standardization

**www.isoiec20000certification.com**
ISO/IEC 20000 certification and qualification schemes

**www.itil-officialsite.com**
The official ITIL® website

**www.itsmf.co.uk**
The IT Service Management Forum

**www.itsmfi.org**
*it*SMF International

**www.sarbanes-oxley.com**
Sarbanes-Oxley

**www.sei.cmu.edu/cmmi/**
Carnegie Mellon University Capability and Maturity Model

# PREFACE

We have written this book with the primary purpose of introducing the IT service management concepts in an easy-to-read style for those looking for more information about service management and how it can be used to improve IT performance in general and the delivery of services to customers in particular.

There are a number of service management 'frameworks'; the two most popular being ITIL and COBIT. In addition, ISO/IEC 20000 offers an international service management standard against which organisations can choose to be audited. ITIL, COBIT and ISO/IEC 20000 offer one or more levels of qualification, the base level in each case being 'Foundation.' Someone looking to study and pass their Foundation level exam in any of these would be expected to be familiar with the basic concepts such as processes, functions and roles that we describe herein.

The reader will therefore find that the contents of this book are entirely consistent with a Foundation level of understanding of service management and thus could find this book relevant to their preparation for sitting a service management foundation level examination.

In writing this book our approach is unique: we have used our collective and extensive real-life experience of working with organisations in this field as both employees and consultants to explain the service management concepts and principles by writing a narrative to explain the subject using real-life examples to which we can all relate.

If you're a Foundation-level examination candidate, this is invaluable because now you won't have to rely only on your memory to answer the questions but can work out the answers from a position of understanding.

If you're looking for an overview of service management, you can acquire this by reading whichever sections interest you in pretty much any order in convenient chunks of time. In this way, the book acts as both a tutorial and a reference guide.

This new edition is fully updated to reflect the latest advice on service management and therefore includes guidance on the new ITIL processes of business relationship management, design coordination and transition planning and support. Needless to say, it is also aligned to the updated Foundation syllabus.

Our use of plain English and the inclusion of real-life examples are all designed to help you, the reader, gain a rapid, clear and insightful understanding of the basic principles, terminology and benefits of service management. Whether this is in the context of your Foundation exam or simply learning about service management, we hope our book is useful and informative.

*Ernest Brewster*
*Richard Griffiths*
*Aidan Lawes*
*John Sansbury*

# INTRODUCTION

## HOW TO USE THIS BOOK

This book covers everything you need to know in order to pass the Service Management Foundation exam. However, we also recognise that many people simply want to understand service management without necessarily taking the exam itself. This book caters for both needs through its simple four-section structure.

- **Section 1:** An overview that introduces the basic concepts of service management and good practice, the service management framework, the service lifecycle and some of the key service management concepts such as processes, functions and roles.

- **Section 2:** A view of each of the five stages of the service lifecycle from service strategy to continual service improvement. Each chapter contains an easy-to-read summary of the core elements of that part of the lifecycle.

- **Section 3:** The core of the book with a chapter describing each of the service management processes and functions.

- **Section 4:** Guidance on measurement and metrics, and the Deming improvement cycle.

In addition, the Appendix contains some useful exam techniques.

Naturally we suggest you start by reading Section 1, but, after that, we have designed each chapter to be self-contained and capable of being read in any sequence and without reference to other chapters. Each chapter can be read in 5–10 minutes.

# SECTION 1:
# OVERVIEW

# 1  WHAT IS SERVICE MANAGEMENT?

## INTRODUCTION

In order to understand what service management is and why it is so important to enterprises, we need to understand what services are and how service management can help service providers to deliver and manage these services.

A service is defined as follows:

### SERVICE

A service is essentially a means of delivering value to customers. This is done by facilitating outcomes that customers want to achieve without the ownership of specific costs and risks.

The outcomes that customers want to achieve are the reason why they purchase or use a service. Typically this will be expressed as a specific business objective (e.g. to enable customers of a bank to perform all transactions and account management activities online or to deliver state services to citizens in a cost-effective manner). The value of the service to the customer is directly dependent on how well a service facilitates these outcomes.

Although the enterprise retains responsibility for managing the overall costs of the business, they often wish to devolve responsibility for owning and managing defined aspects to an internal or external entity that has acknowledged expertise in the area.

This is a generic concept that applies to the purchase of any service. Consider financial planning. As a customer, we recognise that we don't have the expertise, or the time, or the inclination to handle all the day-to-day decision-making and management of individual investments that are required. Therefore, we engage the services of a professional manager to provide us a service. As long as their performance delivers a value (increasing wealth) at a price that we believe is reasonable, we are happy to let them invest in all the necessary systems and processes that are needed for the wealth creation activities.

In the past, service providers often focused on the technical (supply side) view of what constituted a service, rather than on the consumption side. Hence it was not unusual for the service provider and the consumer to have different definitions and perceptions of what services were provided, or for the provider to know all about the cost of individual components, but not the total cost of a service that the consumer understood.

Service management is what enables a service provider to:

- understand the services that they are providing from both a consumer and provider perspective;
- ensure that the services really do facilitate the outcomes that their customers want to achieve;
- understand the value of those services to their customers and hence their relative importance;
- understand and manage all of the costs and risks associated with providing those services.

### SERVICE MANAGEMENT

Service management is a set of specialised organisational capabilities for providing value to customers in the form of services.

These 'specialised organisational capabilities' include the processes, activities, functions and roles that a service provider uses in delivering services to their customers, as well as the ability to establish suitable organisation structures, manage knowledge and understand how to facilitate outcomes that create value.

Although there is no single definition of a profession, it is widely accepted that the word profession applies where a group of people share common standards and disciplines based on a high level of knowledge and skills, which are gained from organised education schemes supported by training through experience and are measured and recognised through formal qualifications. Moreover, a profession seeks to use its influence through the development of good practice guidance and advice in order to improve the standard of performance in its given field.

Service management has a clear right to regard itself as a profession, and the exercise of service management disciplines as professional practice is performed and supported by a global community drawn from all market sectors. There is a rich body of knowledge and experience including formal schemes for the education of individuals.

## 'BEST PRACTICE' VERSUS 'GOOD PRACTICE'

Enterprises operating in dynamic environments need to improve their performance and maintain competitive advantage. Adopting practices in industry-wide use can help to improve capability.

The term 'best practice' generally refers to the 'best possible way of doing something'. As a concept, it was first raised as long ago as 1919, but it was popularised in the 1980s through Tom Peters' books on business management.

The idea behind best practice is that one creates a specification for what is accepted by a wide community as being the best approach for any given situation. Then, one can compare actual job performance against these best practices and determine whether the job performance was lacking in quality somehow. Alternatively, the specification for best practices may need updating to include lessons learned from the job performance being graded.

Enterprises should not be trying to 'implement' any specific best practice, but adapting and adopting it to suit their specific requirements. In doing this, they may also draw upon other sources of good practice, such as public standards and frameworks, or the proprietary knowledge of individuals and other enterprises. More recently, the ITIL framework has offered a supplementary list as illustrated in Figure 1.1.

**Figure 1.1 Sources of good practice**

| Traditional ITIL | Updated ITIL |
| --- | --- |
| • Public frameworks (e.g. COBIT, Six Sigma, CMMI, Prince2) | • Academic research |
| • Standards (e.g. ISO/IEC 20000, ISO 9001, ISO/IEC 27001 | • Industry practices |
| • Proprietary knowledge (i.e. within an organisation) | • Training and education |
| | • Internal experience |

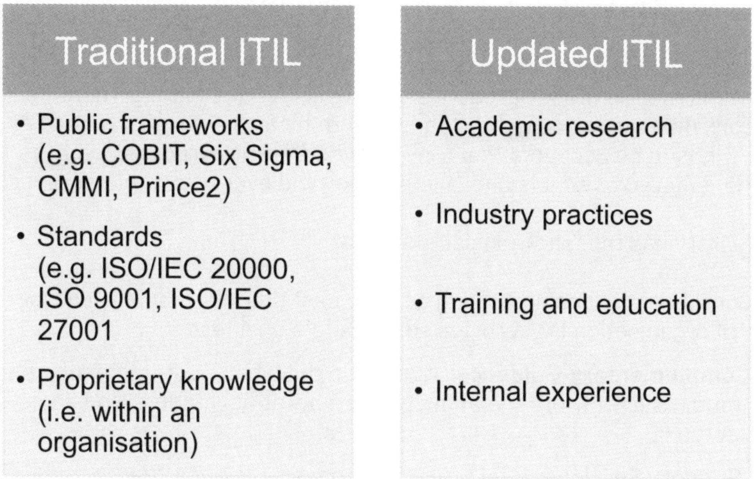

These sources have different characteristics:

- Public frameworks and standards have been validated across diverse environments.
- Knowledge of them is widely distributed among industry professionals.
- Training and certification programmes are publicly available.
- The acquisition of knowledge through the labour market is more readily achievable.

The proprietary knowledge of enterprises and individuals is usually customised for the local context and specific business needs of an organisation. It may only be available to a wider market under commercial terms and may be poorly documented and hard to extract. If embedded within individuals it may not be documented at all.

Enterprises deploying solutions based on good and best practice should, in theory, have an optimal and unique solution. Their solution may include ideas that are gradually adopted by other enterprises and, having been widely accepted, eventually become recognised inputs to good and best practice.

## THE ITIL FRAMEWORK

ITIL is not a standard in the formal sense but a framework which is a source of good practice in service management. The standard for IT service management (ITSM) is ISO/IEC 20000, which is aligned with, but not dependent on, ITIL.

As a formal standard, ISO/IEC 20000 defines a set of requirements against which an organisation can be independently audited and, if they satisfy those requirements, can be certificated to that effect. The requirements focus on what must be achieved rather than how that is done. ITIL provides guidance about how different aspects of the solution can be developed.

The International Organization for Standardization (ISO) and Axelos, with the cooperation of the independent user group *it*SMF (the IT Service Management Forum), have publicly committed to keeping the standard and the framework as aligned as possible. However, it has to be accepted that they serve different purposes and have their own development lifecycles so it is unlikely that they will ever be completely synchronised.

The ITIL Library has the following components:

- **ITIL Core:** Publications describing generic best practice that is applicable to all types of organisation that provide services to a business.
- **ITIL Complementary Guidance:** A set of publications with guidance specific to industry sectors, organisation types, operating models and technology architectures.
- **Web Support Services:** Interactive web-based facilities that include a self-assessment process maturity model (co-built by one of this book's authors).

The objective of the ITIL service management framework is to provide guidance applicable to all types of organisations that provide IT services to businesses, irrespective of their size, complexity, or whether they are commercial service providers or internal divisions of a business. The framework shouldn't be bureaucratic or unwieldy provided it is used sensibly and in full recognition of the business needs of the specific enterprise.

ITIL-based solutions have been deployed successfully around the world for nearly 30 years. Over this time, the framework has evolved considerably. The original publications, of which there were over 40, tended to be single topic and function-based. The next iteration reduced the number of books considerably, taking a process-based view and concatenating topics to reinforce the integrated nature of service management solutions. The latest iteration, the 2011 Edition, now provides a broader, holistic service lifecycle approach.

The generic nature of ITIL is both a strength and a weakness. Since it is generic, it truly can be applied to any organisation of any size in any market sector and regardless of whether the service provider is internal to the business or a commercial enterprise. However, organisations have to adopt and adapt the guidance that it contains to their specific requirements, which in some cases requires considerable effort and commitment.

Unfortunately, much of the focus in learning programmes is on the specifics of terminology and process definitions included within the ITIL volumes, which means that individuals aren't always equipped to make the necessary decisions about how to implement key processes and functions. Organisations should not be seeking to 'implement ITIL', but to implement a service management solution based on ITIL that meets the needs of the organisation.

## THE ITIL CORE

The service lifecycle is an approach to IT service management that emphasises the importance of coordination and control across the various functions, processes and systems necessary to manage the full lifecycle of IT services. The service management lifecycle approach considers the strategy, design, transition, operation and continual improvement of IT services. The service lifecycle is described in a set of five publications within the ITIL Core set. Each of these publications covers a stage of the service lifecycle (see Figure 1.2) from the initial definition and analysis of business requirements in service strategy (SS) and service design (SD), through migration into the live environment within service transition (ST), to live operation and improvement in service operation (SO) and continual service improvement (CSI). The term 'continual' is used in preference to 'continuous' to emphasise that this activity is not performed on a constant basis, but as a series of planned and controlled actions.

**Figure 1.2  The service lifecycle**

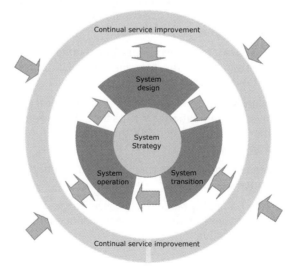

Service strategy is the hub around which everything revolves. Strategy drives all the decisions that are subsequently taken. Design, transition and operation are the more iterative cyclic activities. At all stages throughout the lifecycle, opportunities arise for improvement.

## COMPLEMENTARY MATERIAL

Although the material in the core is likely to remain fairly constant, complementary material is likely to be more dynamic. Complementary material may take the form of books or web-based material and may be sourced from the wider industry.

Examples of such material are glossary of terms, process models, process templates, role descriptions, case studies, targeted overviews and study aids for passing examinations.

Other publications that focus on specific market sectors, techniques or technologies are more likely to be produced by organisations such as *it*SMF or by the vendor community.

## RELATED MATERIAL

Apart from the ISO/IEC 20000 standard, ITIL is also complementary to many other standards, frameworks and approaches. No one of these items will provide everything that an enterprise will wish to use in developing and managing their business. The secret is to draw on them for their insight and guidance as appropriate. Among the many such complementary approaches are:

- **Balanced scorecard:** A management tool developed by Dr Robert Kaplan and Dr David Norton. A balanced scorecard enables a strategy to be broken down into key performance indicators (KPIs). Performance against the KPIs is used to demonstrate how well the strategy is being achieved. A balanced scorecard has four major areas, each of which are considered at different levels of detail throughout the organisation.
- **COBIT:** Control OBjectives for Information and related Technology provides guidance and best practice for the management of IT processes. COBIT is published by the IT Governance Institute.
- **CMMI-SVC:** Capability Maturity Model Integration is a process improvement approach that gives organisations the essential elements for effective process improvement. CMMI-SVC is a variant aimed at service establishment, management and delivery.
- **EFQM:** The European Foundation for Quality Management is a framework for organisational management systems.
- **eSCM–SP:** eSourcing Capability Model for Service Providers is a framework to help IT service providers develop their IT service management capabilities from a service sourcing perspective.

- **ISO 9000:** A generic quality management standard, with which ISO/IEC 20000 is aligned.
- **ISO/IEC 19770:** Software Asset Management standard, which is aligned with ISO/IEC 20000.
- **ISO/IEC 27001:** ISO Specification for Information Security Management. The corresponding code of practice is ISO/IEC 17799.
- **Lean:** a production practice centred around creating more value with less work.
- **PRINCE2:** The standard UK government methodology for project management.
- **SOX:** the Sarbanes–Oxley framework for corporate governance.
- **Six Sigma:** a business management strategy, initially implemented by Motorola, which today enjoys widespread application in many sectors of industry.

Each of these contributes something different, as can be surmised from the brief descriptions, whether it be as legislation to comply with, as a standard to aspire to or as a method of measuring success. Enterprises globally have developed total corporate solutions embracing many permutations of these approaches.

## THE ITIL SERVICE MANAGEMENT MODEL

Whether services are being provided by an internal unit of the organisation or contracted to an external agency, all services should be driven solely by business needs and judged by the value that they provide to the organisation. Decision-making therefore rests with the business. Within this context, services must also reflect the defined strategies and policies of the service provider organisation, which is particularly significant for external providers.

Figure 1.3 illustrates how the service lifecycle is initiated from a change in requirements at the business level. These new or changed requirements are identified and agreed at the service strategy stage and documented. Each of these 'packages' will have an associated defined set of business outcomes.

The package is passed to the service design stage where a service solution is produced, defining everything necessary to take this service through the remaining stages of the lifecycle. Solutions may be developed internally or consist of bought-in components that are integrated internally.

The design definition is passed to the service transition stage, where the service is built, evaluated, tested, validated and transitioned into the live environment, where it enters the live service operation stage. The transition phase is also responsible for support-ing the service in its early life and the phasing out of any services that are no longer required.

Service operation focuses on providing effective and efficient operational services to deliver the required business outcomes and value to the customer. This is where any value is actually delivered and measured.

**Figure 1.3  Key activities of the service lifecycle stages**

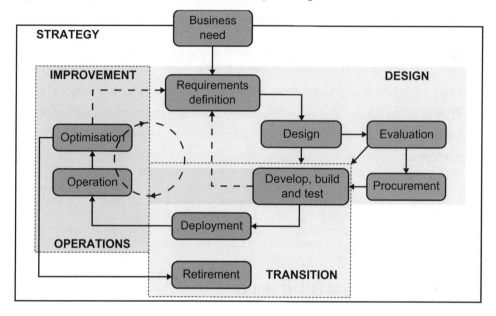

Continual service improvement identifies opportunities for improvement (which may arise anywhere within any of the lifecycle stages) based on measurement and reporting of the efficiency, effectiveness, cost-effectiveness and compliance of the services themselves, the technology that is in use and the service management processes used to manage these components. Although the measurements are taken during the operational phase, improvements may be identified for any phase of the lifecycle.

## KEY CONCEPTS

### Value

From the earlier definition of a service, it is clear that the primary focus is on delivering value to the service consumer. Value is created through providing the right service under the right conditions.

Customers value an IT service when they see a clear relationship between that IT service and the business value that they need to generate. In the past, both IT and business management have been very poor at understanding this link: IT has often known all about the costs of components, but not the cost of providing a service that the business understands, and the business has been unable to make value-based decisions about the worth of such solutions.

Value is created through two components:

- **Utility:** Value in the form of what the customer gets from the service. This will either be from providing new business lines or from the relaxation of existing constraints on the customer's ability to achieve their desired outcomes. Utility is about what the product or service does, determining whether it is 'fit for purpose'.

- **Warranty:** Value in the form of how this 'utility' is delivered to the customer. This is seen as the positive effect of the service being available when and where it is required, in sufficient capacity to meet the business needs, and being sufficiently reliable in terms of continuity and security for it to be depended on (i.e. it is 'fit for use').

## UTILITY

Functionality offered by a product or service to meet a particular need. Utility is often summarised as 'what it does'.

## WARRANTY

A promise or guarantee that a product or service will meet its agreed requirements.

Neither utility nor warranty can deliver full value on its own. A product or service may do exactly what the customer requires, but if it performs poorly, or is unavailable, insecure or unreliable, it cannot deliver maximum value. Conversely, a service will not deliver value if it does not provide the functionality needed, even though it may be highly available, reliable and secure and offer high levels of performance.

Value is only created when both utility and warranty are satisfied. A service that seems potentially attractive on paper to a customer in terms of the utility that it offers won't be perceived as providing real value if the way it is delivered is highly unreliable or it is delivered in an insecure manner. A customer's ability to realise value from an IT service is dependent on both the utility associated with the service and the degree to which they can rely on the consistent delivery of that service (the service warranty).

## EXAMPLE

When ATMs were introduced, they removed the time constraint of customers being able to withdraw cash from their account only when the bank branch was open. Since their introduction, further functionality has been added (account balances, mini statements, bill payment etc.). These are all aspects of utility, but they are of course useless unless ATMs are sited in convenient locations, are kept topped up with cash and printer paper, have secure access controls and are reliable.

Internet banking offered new utility through additional functions (e.g. transfers and online account creation) as well as allowing the customer to do all these anytime, anywhere. Different security, capacity and availability aspects are required in order to ensure the functionality is provided.

## Service assets

Service providers create value through using their assets in the form of resources and capabilities.

### RESOURCES

A generic term that includes IT infrastructure, people, money or anything else that might help to deliver an IT service. Resources are considered to be assets of an organisation.

### CAPABILITIES

The ability of an organisation, person, process, application, configuration item or IT service to carry out an activity. Capabilities are intangible assets of an organisation.

The key difference between resource assets and capability assets is that, typically, resources can be purchased in the marketplace while distinctive capabilities can only be developed over time. Capabilities reflect the knowledge and experience of the organisation and are used to transform physical resources into services. The distinctive capabilities of a service provider, often quite intangible, set it apart from its competitors and enable it to attract and retain customers by offering unique value propositions.

The business unit to which the service is provided will also have resources and capabilities that are harnessed to provide the end service to the customer. The integration between the service and the business unit's own assets may be very tight, making it hard to distinguish between the two, or it may be much more clearly separated.

Figure 1.4 shows the role of service assets in delivering business value through services.

## Service model

A service model describes how a service provider creates value for a given portfolio of customer contracts by connecting the demand for service from the assets of its customers with the service provider's service assets. It describes both the structure and the dynamics of the service:

- **Structure:** The particular service assets needed to deliver the service and the patterns in which they are configured.
- **Dynamics:** The activities, flow of resources, coordination and interactions between customer and service provider assets (e.g. interaction between service users and service agents). Service dynamics include patterns of business activity (PBAs), demand patterns, exceptions and variations.

**Figure 1.4  Service delivery through service assets**

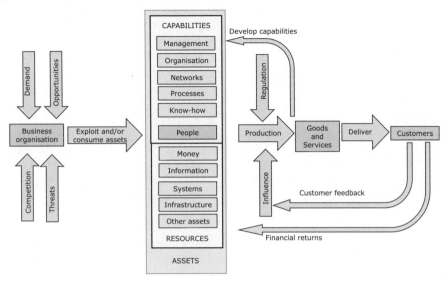

A service model may include:

- process maps;
- workflow diagrams;
- queuing models;
- activity patterns.

Once defined, variants of a service model can be generated in order to tailor a service to a customer's specific needs.

### Functions, processes and roles

The terms function, process and role are often confused. This is not surprising since they are so intertwined. In addition, the way the words are used in ITIL is precise and may be confused with the way these words are used in a more general context.

**FUNCTION**

A self-contained unit of an organisation that carries out one or more processes or activities (e.g. the service desk or IT operations).

In this context a function is a structural part of an organisation (e.g. a division or a business unit) established to do specific things. For example, the service desk is a function that is created to perform defined activities and produce specified outcomes. To be

13

'self-contained', the service desk typically requires a toolset, one or more forms of communication (such as a telephone), some knowledge and training, and desks and chairs, among other necessities. People within a function have defined roles that they perform to deliver the outcomes required. By their nature, functions are specialised and have their own disciplines, skills, performance measures and knowledge base. Functions perform activities that are elements of processes. Individual functions may perform an entire process or, quite commonly, share processes with other functions.

---

### PROCESS

A process is a set of activities and procedures intended to achieve a specific objective. A process may include any of the roles, responsibilities, tools and management controls required to meet the objectives reliably. A process may define policies, standards, guidelines, activities and work instructions if they are needed.

---

A process consists of a set of coordinated activities using resources and capabilities to produce an outcome, which, directly or indirectly, creates value for an external customer or stakeholder.

## Process characteristics

Every process consists of a number of elements, as shown in Figure 1.5. A process takes inputs and transforms them, using the appropriate enablers, to produce the required outputs in a closed-loop system that allows for feedback and improvement. Process control ensures that consistent repeatable processes are established, regulated and managed so that their performance is effective and efficient.

Figure 1.5 illustrates some of the basic features of a process. First, a process, initiated by an event or trigger, transforms inputs into outputs through a series of activities carried out by people or systems with specific roles with procedures or work instructions. It makes use of organisational resources and capabilities as process enablers. It has an owner responsible for it. It has documented policy, terms of reference and objectives, and it is controlled to ensure it meets its specified purpose. The process is measured against defined metrics to determine how effectively it is operating and the results are fed back to drive continual improvement (this is what is known as a closed-loop feedback system).

In line with this, all processes will have certain characteristics:

- **Measurable:** We must be able to measure the process. The performance of the process is incredibly important. Managers will want to measure the cost and quality. People involved operationally with the process are concerned with how long it takes and how easy it is to use.

- **Specific results:** A process exists in order to deliver a specific result, which must be identifiable and countable.

**Figure 1.5 Process structure**

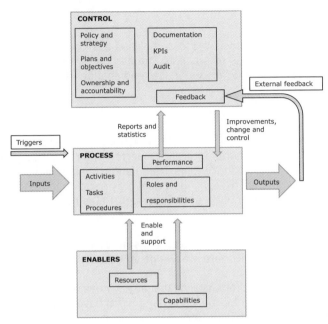

- **Customers:** Each process delivers its main results to a customer or stakeholder, who may be internal or external, and the results must meet their expectations.

- **Responds to a specific event:** Each process, whether it is ongoing or iterative, will have a specific trigger.

---

**EXAMPLE**

Let's use a process for booking theatre tickets by telephone as an example:

- **Measurement:** Management will want to ensure quality (e.g. bookings are correctly recorded, seats aren't 'double booked' etc.). The staff taking the bookings by phone may want a system that remembers details of customers from previous transactions, thus making it easier to use.

- **Results:** Each correct set of theatre tickets despatched on time or made available for collection might be the result.

- **Customer:** Customer expectations may be that the process makes it easy to book tickets and that they are either received before they go to see the show or are available at the box office on arrival.

- **Trigger:** The customer telephone call.

## Roles

> **ROLE**
>
> A set of responsibilities, activities and authorities assigned to a person or team. A role is defined in a process or function. One person or team may have multiple roles (e.g. the roles of configuration manager and change manager may be carried out by a single person).

Therefore, a role describes what an individual actually does. Every organisation will define those roles that it requires in order to perform the necessary tasks and will allocate individuals to perform those roles. The relationship between roles and persons is a many-to-many relationship (i.e. an individual may perform more than one role and a role may be performed by more than one person). Roles may or may not be related to job titles.

As stated earlier, there should be one role that is accountable for any specific task or process. In the ITIL framework, there are five generic roles:

**Process owner** – accountable for ensuring that all activities within a process are undertaken. Since they are accountable, only one person can have this role within an organisation. The person has responsibility for:

- defining the process strategy;
- assisting with the design of the process;
- ensuring that process documentation is available and current, and that all staff are trained correctly;
- defining policies and standards to be followed;
- defining KPIs and auditing to ensure that the process is being followed correctly and is effective and efficient;
- reviewing proposed enhancements and providing input to the service improvement plan.

**Process manager** or **managers** – responsible for the operational management of a process including:

- ensuring the successful conduct of process activities;
- management of the process practitioners undertaking process roles;
- managing process resource requirements;
- monitoring and reporting on process performance;
- identifying and promoting process improvement opportunities and entering these in the CSI register.

**Process practitioners** – responsible for carrying out one or more process activities including:

- working with other stakeholders to ensure their own contributions are effective;
- validating and ensuring the integrity of process inputs, outputs and interfaces for their process(es);
- creating or updating records to show that activities have been carried out correctly.

**Service owner** – accountable to the customer for a particular service. As with the process owner, having accountability for the service means there can be only one IT service owner per service, although in practice the ultimate authority sits with the business service owner. The IT service owner is responsible for:

- acting as the prime customer contact for all service-related enquiries and issues, and as an escalation point for major incidents;
- representing the service in change advisory board (CAB) and customer meetings;
- participating in negotiating SLAs and OLAs, and ensuring the service is correctly defined in the service catalogue;
- ensuring that the service is delivered as agreed (i.e. service levels are met);
- identifying opportunities for improving the service provided;
- ensuring that effective service monitoring is implemented.

**Service manager** or **managers** – responsible for the operational management of services. This is a generic term for any manager within the service provider.

One reason why people get confused about processes and functions is that it is common to give names to organisational units that are the same as the names of processes. For example, change management is an SM process, but many organisations will have a function or team called change management with responsibility for the change management process. It is important to recognise that organisational structures are a matter of choice, but irrespective of how the organisation is structured and what the elements are called, the service management processes are not a matter of choice.

### The interrelationship between functions, process and roles

Figure 1.6 illustrates the typical interrelationship between the three entities. Processes can span one or more functions and require activities to be performed by one or more roles within any function. In fact, it is usually even more complex than this, since each role may have a different type of engagement in any individual process.

### Authority matrix

An authority matrix is often used within organisations to indicate specific roles and responsibilities in relation to processes and activities.

**Figure 1.6 Functions, roles and processes**

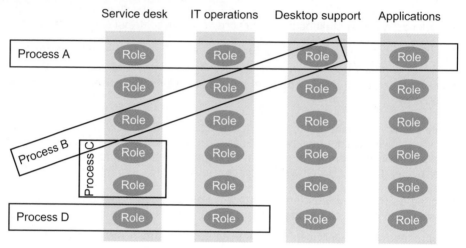

The RACI model is an example of an authority matrix. It is used to map the process activities to the roles involved in their execution. The acronym RACI is derived from the distinct ways a role can be involved in a process.

| **R**esponsible | executes the process or activity | (does the work) |
| **A**ccountable | has ownership of quality and the end result | (ultimate owner) |
| **C**onsulted | provides input of knowledge and information | (provides assistance) |
| **I**nformed | receives information about execution | (needs to know) |

Within the RACI model, each activity must have a role identified as accountable and responsible, whereas consulted and informed are optional. There must be only one accountable role for each activity.

Generic roles are normally used in the RACI model, but it is vitally important that the role–activity links it describes are mapped back to specific individuals within the organisation.

Separating the role involvement from the organisation allows flexibility in the application of role–activity relationships to the realities and constraints of organisational design:

- It recognises that the same process (or activity) may be carried out by more than one organisational role or unit.

- It allows organisation design to change without impacting the underlying process model.

- It recognises constraints of geographically diverse organisations which may have to combine many responsibilities in fewer roles in smaller sites.

- It allows for complex organisations covering diverse businesses to adopt the same underlying process model without extensive adaptation.

## ITIL processes and functions

Table 1.1 lists the ITIL service management processes and functions in alphabetical order, identifying the lifecycle stage in which they sit and the chapter in Section 3 that contains greater detail. Most processes play a role during each subsequent lifecycle stage, but only significant references are included. The shaded processes are not part of the service management foundation syllabus and are not covered in detail in this book except for demand management which includes the concept of 'patterns of business activity' which remains within the syllabus.

**Table 1.1  ITIL service management processes and functions**

| Service management process/function | Service lifecycle stage | Section 3 chapter |
| --- | --- | --- |
| Seven-step improvement process | CSI | 32 |
| Access management | SO | 18 |
| Application management | SO | 30 |
| Availability management | SD | 16 |
| Business relationship management | SS | 7 |
| Capacity management | SD | 15 |
| Change evaluation | ST | (See p.35.) |
| Change management | ST | 22 |
| Demand management | SS | 9 |
| Design coordination | SD | 11 |
| Event management | SO | 29 |
| Financial management for IT services | SS | 8 |
| Incident management | SO | 26 |
| Information security management | SD | 18 |
| IT operations management | SO | 28 |
| IT service continuity management | SD | 17 |
| Knowledge management | ST | 20 |
| Problem management | SO | 27 |
| Management of organisational and stakeholder change | ST | (See p.36.) |

*(Continued)*

19

**Table 1.1 (Continued)**

| Service management process/function | Service lifecycle stage | Section 3 chapter |
|---|---|---|
| Release and deployment management | ST | 23 |
| Request fulfilment | SO | 25 |
| Service asset and configuration | ST | 21 |
| Service catalogue management | SD | 12 |
| Service desk | SO | 24 |
| Service level management | SD | 13 |
| Service measurement | CSI | 33 |
| Service portfolio management | SS | 10 |
| Service reporting | CSI | 33 |
| Service validation and testing | ST | (See p.35.) |
| Strategy management for IT services | SS | 19 |
| Supplier management | SD | 14 |
| Technical management | SO | 31 |
| Transition planning and support | ST | 19 |

# SECTION 2:
# THE SERVICE LIFECYCLE

# 2 SERVICE STRATEGY

## INTRODUCTION

The objective of service strategy is to offer better services than the competition. You need to beat the opposition to survive. Of course, to be successful in the longer term, as the industrial landscape adjusts to the inevitable economic, social, technological and political changes, organisations have to think long term. So service strategy is not just about the strategy for individual services today, but also about positioning the IT service provider for the long haul. It also includes the design, development and implementation of service management as a foundation for sound governance and as part of the organisation's strategic asset base.

## GOVERNANCE

The concept of governance is central to the sound operation and management of all healthy organisations. It covers the various policies, processes and structures established by senior management to ensure the smooth running and effective control of the organisation. The guidance provided through the ITIL processes offers a sound foundation for the development of effective governance, which is as important to the IT provider as to any other organisation.

The international standard for IT governance, ISO/IEC 38500:2008, 'provides a framework for effective governance of IT to assist those at the highest level of organisations to understand and fulfil their legal, regulatory and ethical obligations in respect of their organisations' use of IT'. This framework sets out six principles for good corporate governance of IT, covering responsibility, strategy, acquisition, performance, conformance and human behaviour, making it clear that IT governance is about much more than IT processes and controls. It is a management system used by directors of an organisation to ensure the proper and effective stewardship of the IT resources.

Nevertheless, effective IT procedures and controls are a vital component of good governance. The ITIL framework can be a key part of the foundations for excellent IT governance.

IT is a service business and the adoption of good service management practices is an effective way to address IT governance. Every part of the service lifecycle has a role to play. For example, service strategy ensures that IT investments not only address issues that are important to the business, but also that they are sound investments that take proper account of costs, benefits and risks. Continual service improvement helps the business achieve greater value and higher levels of efficiency while conforming to standards such as ISO/IEC 20000 and external constraints such as Sarbanes–Oxley (SOX). Further specific references to IT governance can be found in Chapter 8 Financial Management for IT Services (a service strategy process) and Chapter 18 Information Security Management and Access Management (service design and service operation processes).

## RISK

The effective management of risk, an important issue for all successful organisations, is a key component of governance.

> ### RISK
>
> An event that could cause damage or loss, or affect the ability to meet objectives. Risk can also be defined as the uncertainty of outcome.

Effective risk management requires a consistent framework in which risks are identified and analysed and appropriate measures put in place to deal with them.

## KEY PROCESSES

The key processes in service strategy are:

- business relationship management (see Chapter 7);
- financial management for IT services (see Chapter 8).
- service portfolio management (see Chapter 10);

## IT SERVICE PROVIDER TYPES

It is important to recognise that there are different types of IT service provider and that although all will have things in common in relation to service management, there will be unique aspects, for example those concerning the commercial relationship with customers and the business served by the provider.

In practice, there is a tremendous variation in the types of IT service provider. Different providers are characterised by their relationship with customers and their positioning in relation to the business or businesses they service. It is helpful to simplify this complexity and identify a small number of provider types that represent the wider variety in the marketplace. This simplification leads to the following three types:

- **Type I – Internal service provider:** This is the in-house IT unit typically positioned within the business units they serve, although it is common for these smaller scale IT units to be consolidated into a corporate IT department that has to balance the interests, demands and priorities of the corporate organisation against those of individual business units.

- **Type II – Shared services unit:** This is where a range of functions, regarded as non-core to the business, are grouped together into a corporate shared service unit. The functions involved are typically IT, Finance and HR, sometimes with legal service, logistics and facilities management.
- **Type III – External service provider:** This is a separate commercial entity from the businesses it services and operates as a competitive business in the marketplace.

## THE FOUR Ps OF STRATEGY

Having considered the IT service provider's strategic approach to the marketplace, the next part of the strategic equation is the IT service provider's approach to service strategy. This may be analysed in terms of the four Ps:

- Strategy as a **Perspective:** This relates to vision, direction and the IT service provider's philosophy for doing business with its customers.
- Strategy as a **Position:** This describes strategy in terms of the IT service provider's general approach to its service offerings (e.g. high value or low cost, emphasis on utility or warranty).
- Strategy as a **Plan:** This describes strategy as a plan showing how the IT service provider will move from where it is today to where it wants to be.
- Strategy as a **Pattern:** This describes strategy as a consistent way of making decisions.

## SERVICE MANAGEMENT AS A STRATEGIC ASSET

There are two components of service strategy. Service strategy is clearly about developing strategies for the delivery of specific services, but there is also the development of service management as a competence for providing services as part of the business strategy and as a basis for good governance.

The development of service management as a strategic asset is central to service strategy.

### STRATEGIC ASSET

Strategic assets are assets that provide the basis for core competence, distinctive performance, durable advantage and qualifications to participate in business opportunities. IT organisations can use the guidance provided by ITIL to transform their service management capabilities into strategic assets.

Service management provides the framework within which value is delivered to the customer in the shape of specific services represented collectively in the service catalogue. The customer's confidence in commissioning new service offerings depends on the service management capabilities of the IT service provider.

## DEVELOPING STRATEGY FOR SPECIFIC SERVICES

In terms of the development of a strategy for a specific service offering, the key elements are concerned with a series of activities that involve:

- understanding the customer and the ways IT can deliver value to them;
- understanding the outcomes the customer wants from the service and how the service will deliver benefit;
- defining critical success factors for the service;
- developing a specification based on the outcomes required by the customer, including the utility and warranty required;
- developing through demand management an understanding of the customer's priorities in relation to patterns of business activity (PBAs).

It is important to remember that individual services have to operate in a broader context. New services must fit into the framework of existing services and any other new services with which they will likely share common services and compete for resources. The development of a service strategy has to take this fully into account.

At an early stage in the development of the service strategy, the initial, conceptual details of the new service will be captured in the service portfolio and the new service will begin its journey through its lifecycle. Through service portfolio management, the new service offering will be put into the broader context of other services, business trends, regulation, the developing marketplace, emerging technologies, competition, risks and so on. The business case, developed in conjunction with financial management, will reflect these factors and explain why the service strategy developed represents the best way forward as well as describing how and to what extent it will deliver value.

The outcome of the service strategy process is a decision to continue with the service or not. Approved services are 'chartered' at which point they are ready to move forward to service design. The transfer into service design requires the production of a service package, which describes in detail the IT service to be delivered to the customer, including the service levels to be achieved and the supporting services that will underpin its delivery.

### SERVICE PACKAGE

A service package comprises two or more services combined to offer a solution to a specific type of customer requirement or to support specific business outcomes. A service package can include a combination of core services, enabling services and enhancing services, and provides specific levels of utility and warranty.

## SERVICE ASSETS

In delivering a service, the IT service provider exploits its own assets to add value to the customer's assets and generate value for the organisation.

The assets used by the IT service provider can be described in terms of its capabilities and resources, which were first introduced in Chapter 1. The development of a successful service strategy needs to be built on an understanding of the service assets that can be brought into play in service delivery. There is no point in formulating a service strategy that requires service assets that will not be available. Making assumptions about the organisation's ability to improve its service asset base, especially its capabilities, introduces an element of risk that needs to be acknowledged, understood and managed.

**Figure 2.1  Generation of value from service and customer assets**

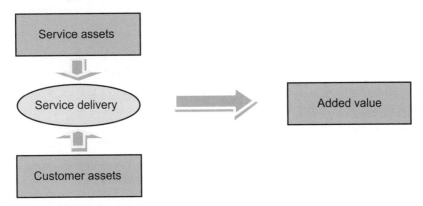

In developing a service strategy it is essential to recognise that generation of value to the business requires a combination of the IT service provider's assets and the customer's assets. This means that the development of service strategy must be informed by knowledge of the customer's resources and capabilities, and the opportunities, threats, vulnerabilities and risks associated with them. The IT service provider must look outwards as well as inwards.

## VALUE

The idea that services add value is fundamental to IT service delivery and is a key input to the development of service strategy. There is little point in developing services that have no recognised value. In Chapter 1, we discussed how value is created through utility or fitness for purpose and warranty or fitness for use. We can measure value not only in terms of quantifiable benefits such as financial savings or increased income, but also in terms of benefits such as service quality, which are less easily quantified and often depend on the perception of the customer or service user. The principle that value depends on customer perception leads us to conclude that effective service strategy requires a way of thinking, a 'marketing mindset', which captures the customer's perspective, through which we can understand both the customer and the outcomes that the customer really values and why, and to what extent they are valued.

## AUTOMATING SERVICE MANAGEMENT PROCESSES

Automating business processes delivers higher utility and warranty thereby generating better performance and value from service and customer assets.

The same applies to IT service management. Earlier in this chapter, we identified IT service management capability as a strategic asset. Building this capability through automation is fundamental to providing value to the business by remaining competitive.

Of course, effective service management in all but the smallest organisations is inconceivable without a level of automation. For example, configuration management based on paper records could hardly deliver in an organisation of any significant scale. Beyond this basic level, we can identify a number of areas where automation can improve capability. For example:

- Monitoring and measuring to an extent not possible by other means, handling high levels of complexity and volume irrespective of time or location.
- Generating automated alerts helps us respond more rapidly to events, helping us maintain service availability.
- Discovery tools enable us to maintain an up-to-date configuration management system and identify and deal with a range of control related problems.
- Sophisticated modelling and simulation helps us design infrastructure and applications, and model complex options for service delivery.
- Artificial intelligence is able to offer a range of capabilities from root cause analysis, through sophisticated alarm and control systems, to complex scheduling and resource management.
- Workflow management systems improve customer service and efficiency across a range of processes.

At a more basic level, automation increases productivity, enables us to handle fluctuating demand and generally do more for less. Critically for IT service management, it also enables us to integrate across different service management processes and functions, for example through improved coherence, shared workflow and escalation processes, shared alarms and alerts, better inter-process communication, information sharing and organisational learning. This improves efficiency, helps reduce errors and duplication of effort, and delivers better value and better service to the customer.

# 3   SERVICE DESIGN

## INTRODUCTION

Once an organisation has determined the IT strategy it wishes to pursue, it uses the service design phase of the lifecycle to create new services which service transition then introduces into the live environment. In so doing, service design aims to take the necessary steps to ensure that the new service will perform as planned and deliver the functionality and benefits intended by the business. This principle is at the heart of the ITIL approach and is why the majority of the service design processes are focused on operational control:

- service catalogue management;
- service level management;
- capacity management;
- design coordination;
- availability management;
- IT service continuity management;
- information security management;
- supplier management.

The contribution that the service design phase of the lifecycle makes can therefore be summarised as ensuring the creation of cost-effective services that provide the level of quality required to satisfy customers and stakeholders throughout the life of the service.

However, the fact that business requirements change over time and generate the need or opportunity for further improvement, means that even an organisation with mature service design processes will need to make changes to services throughout their life. Service design therefore has an important role to play in supporting continual service improvement and is as important for managing changes to existing services as it is in designing new services. In this respect, service design must also consider the impact of its activities on the overall services, systems, architecture, tools and measurements in order to minimise the potential for disruption when a new or changed service is introduced into the live environment.

## WHY SERVICE DESIGN?

Without well-established service design, services will become less stable and more expensive to maintain and become increasingly less supportive of business and customer needs. Furthermore, the cost of correcting these deficiencies is almost always higher than the costs that would have been incurred to prevent them at the design stage.

Not every change will require service design activities. Rather these are reserved for 'significant' changes. Each organisation must decide its own definition of 'significant' and use the change management process to assess the significance of each change and therefore whether or not service design activities need to be used.

Good service design will deliver a range of business benefits that help to underline its importance in the design of new and changed services. These are summarised below:

- Lower cost services because of the lower support and enhancement costs, leading to lower total cost of ownership (TCO).
- Services that consistently provide the required level of quality and alignment to business and customer needs.
- Faster and easier introduction of new services and changes.
- Better governance to ensure compliance to legal and corporate rules and guidelines.
- Better measurement capability to support decision-making and continual improvement.

Poor planning, preparation and management are common reasons for the failure of plans and projects in general and the design and deployment of new and changed services in particular. ITIL helps prevent this by offering guidance on preparing and planning the use of people, processes, products and partners: the Four Ps of service design. (N.B. It is important not to confuse these with the Four Ps of service strategy discussed in Chapter 2.)

## THE FIVE MAJOR ASPECTS OF SERVICE DESIGN

There are five separate aspects of service design that together describe the scope of this part of the service lifecycle:

- The introduction of new or changed services through the accurate identification of business requirements and the agreed definition of service requirements.
- The service management systems and tools such as the service portfolio, ensuring mutual consistency with other services and appropriate tools support.
- The capability of technology architectures and management systems to operate and maintain new services.
- The capability of all processes, not just those in service design, to operate and maintain new and changed services.

- Designing in the appropriate measurement methods and metrics necessary for performance analysis of services, improved decision-making and continual improvement.

## OBJECTIVES OF SERVICE DESIGN

From the considerations above, we can appreciate that the main objectives of service design are:

- to design services that not only satisfy business and stakeholder objectives in terms of quality, ease-of-use, compliance and security, but also minimise the total cost of ownership;
- to design efficient and effective policies, plans, processes, architectures and frameworks to manage services throughout their lifecycle;
- to support service transition in identifying and managing the risks associated with introducing new or changed services;
- to design measurement systems for assessing the efficiency and effectiveness of service design and its deliverables;
- to contribute to continual service improvement (CSI), particularly by designing in features and benefits and then responding to improvement opportunities identified from the operational environment.

## THE SERVICE DESIGN PACKAGE

The design stage takes a set of new or changed business requirements and develops a solution to meet them. The developed solution is passed to service transition to be built, tested and deployed into the live environment.

However, it is not enough simply to pass the technical or architectural design to service transition. The service transition teams will need more than this to deliver a fully functioning service that provides the utility and warranty expected. They need a blueprint that covers all aspects of the new service. This blueprint is known as the service design package.

### SERVICE DESIGN PACKAGE

The document(s) defining all relevant aspects of an IT service together with their requirements through each stage of the service's lifecycle. A service design package is usually produced each time a new IT service is introduced, for major changes to an IT service or for an IT service retirement.

31

The key contents of the service design package include:

- the service definition, agreed business requirements and how and where the service will be used;
- the service design including the architectural design, functional requirements, SLRs/ SLAs (if available), service and operational management requirements including metrics and key performance indicators, supporting services and agreements;
- a service model showing the overall structure and dynamics of the service, showing how customer and service assets, service management functions and processes come together to deliver value;
- an assessment of organisational readiness and its implications;
- a plan covering all stages of the service lifecycle;
- plans for service transition (covering build and assembly, test, release and deployment) and for operational service acceptance;
- acceptance criteria and the strategy and plan for user acceptance testing.

# 4　SERVICE TRANSITION

## INTRODUCTION

There has frequently been a disconnection between the development and operations departments within IT, which has consequently led to many failed implementations of new or changed services. Service transition is concerned with bridging that gap smoothly, ensuring that operational requirements are fully considered and catered for before anything is moved into the live environment, including documentation and training for users and support staff. Service transition is also responsible for the decommissioning and removal of services that are no longer required, and for the transfer of a service from one service provider to another.

Smooth transition is achieved by taking a new or changed service design package (SDP) from the service design stage, testing it to ensure that it correctly meets the needs of the business and deploying it within the production environment.

Some of the processes that are described within this phase are also used within other phases, in particular service knowledge, change and service asset and configuration management.

Figure 4.1 shows the seven processes covered by service transition, along with managing organisational and stakeholder change, which is a key service transition activity.

The ITIL Foundation syllabus only requires detailed knowledge of the five shaded areas in the diagram (i.e. change management, SACM, release and deployment management, knowledge management and transition planning and support), each of which has a separate chapter in Section 3. The remainder are covered later in this chapter.

## PURPOSE AND OBJECTIVES

The purpose of service transition is to:

- set customer expectations on how the new or changed service will enable business change;
- enable the customer to integrate a release seamlessly into their business processes and services;
- reduce variations in the predicted and actual performance of the services once they are introduced;

- reduce known errors and minimise the risks from change;

- ensure that the service can be used in the manner in which it is required.

**Figure 4.1 Service transition processes**

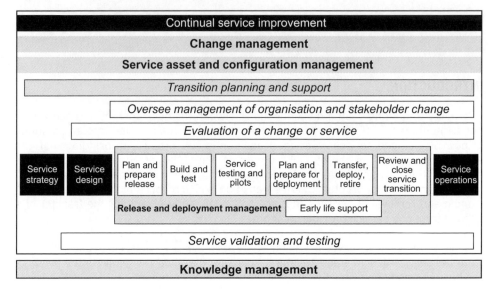

The objectives are to:

- plan and manage the resources to introduce and activate a new or changed service to the live environment within the predicted cost, quality and time estimates;

- minimise any unpredicted impact on the production services, operations and support organisation;

- increase customer, user and service management staff satisfaction with the deployment of new or changed services, including communications, release documentation, training and knowledge transfer;

- increase correct use of the services and any underlying applications and technology solutions;

- provide clear and comprehensive plans that enable alignment between the business and service transition.

Service transition includes the management and coordination of the resources that are needed to package, build, test and deploy a release into production and to establish new or changed services as specified by the customer and stakeholder requirements. Service transition also manages the transfer of services to or from external service providers.

When it is done well, service transition helps organisations to be more agile, with the capability and capacity to respond more rapidly and with greater certainty of success. This ability to adapt makes organisations more competitive as market places adjust to economic, social, environmental and political change.

Mergers, acquisitions and other major organisational changes are better managed, productivity losses through change are minimised, and risks are identified and dealt with. It also underpins sound financial management, as effective planning and budgeting for transition means fewer surprises, less disruption, higher productivity and better management of resources. As an example, in transitions that involve decommissioning of existing systems and services, the organisation will be able to identify opportunities for cost reduction through the timely termination of support contracts, maintenance agreements and licences. Services are better aligned with the needs of the business and, because training needs are identified in transition planning, people know what to expect from new or changed services and are ready to make best use of them.

In summary, effective service transition is an essential part of good governance. Change can be embraced more rapidly and more effectively without damaging the business, and the business, its customers and its employees can all face change with greater confidence in the outcome. Everyone knows what to expect and, if service transition is effective, those expectations will be borne out in reality.

## PROCESS OBJECTIVES AND VALUE

Section 3 contains details on five of the processes in this phase. The remaining two processes and the activity 'managing organisational and stakeholder change' are described briefly below.

### Service validation and testing

The objective of service validation and testing is to ensure that a new or changed service and its associated release process will meet the needs of the business at the agreed cost.

Service validation and testing activities can be applied throughout the service lifecycle to provide quality assurance of any aspect of a service. The complete end-to-end service needs to be considered and both internally and externally developed service components included.

Service validation provides value by preventing service failures that can harm the service provider's and the customer's assets, which can result in outcomes such as loss of reputation, financial loss, time delays, injury or even death.

### Change evaluation

Evaluation is a generic process that considers whether the performance of something is acceptable, value for money, fit for purpose and whether implementation can proceed based on defined and agreed criteria. The objectives of change evaluation are:

- to evaluate the intended effects of a change and as much of the unintended effects as reasonably practical given capacity, resource and organisational constraints;
- to provide good quality outputs from the evaluation process so that change management can expedite an effective decision about whether a change is to be approved or not;
- to set stakeholder expectations correctly.

The scope includes the evaluation of any new or changed service defined by service design, during deployment and before final transition to the production environment.

### Management of organisational and stakeholder change

While service transition's basic role is to implement a new or changed service, a change of any significance may involve an organisational change, ranging from moving a few staff to work from new premises through to major alterations in the nature of business working (e.g. from face-to-face retail to web-based trading).

Organisational change efforts fail or fall short of their goals because changes and transitions are not led, managed and monitored efficiently across the organisation and throughout the change process. Service transition therefore needs to ensure that any such implications are considered and brought to the attention of relevant stakeholders to ensure that the organisation is ready to receive and use the new service when it is introduced.

## CHALLENGES

Establishing effective service transition can be challenging. The following are some of the issues that can arise and need to be managed:

- Ensuring that all change activity is driven through service transition.
- Balancing the evolving needs of the business against the need to protect live services (i.e. being responsive while maintaining suitable protection).
- Integrating with development and project lifecycles which traditionally are independent.
- Having the appropriate authority and empowerment to execute the processes as defined.
- Managing people's perceptions so that the processes are not seen as a barrier to change or as being over bureaucratic.

## ROLES

The service transition manager is responsible for planning and coordinating the resources to deploy a major release within the predicted cost, time and quality estimates.

# 5    SERVICE OPERATION

## INTRODUCTION

Service operation is the phase of the IT service management lifecycle that is responsible for 'business as usual' activities. If services are not utilised or are not delivered efficiently and effectively, they will not deliver their full value, irrespective of how well designed they may be. It is service operation that is responsible for utilising the processes to deliver services to users and customers.

Service operation is where the value that has been modelled in service strategy and confirmed through service design and service transition is actually delivered. Without service operation running the services as designed and utilising the processes as designed, there would be no control and management of the services. Production of meaningful metrics by service operation will form the basis and starting point for service improvement activity.

## PURPOSE AND OBJECTIVES

The purpose of service operation is to organise and conduct the activities and processes needed to deliver services to business users at agreed levels of service. Additionally, service operation is responsible for the ongoing management of the technology (infrastructure and applications) that is utilised to deliver and support the services.

Service operation is a balancing act. It is not just a matter of carrying out the processes on a day-to-day basis. There is a dynamic 'debate' that is taking place on four levels. These are known as the 'four balances of service operation':

- **Internal IT view versus external business view:** The external business view of IT will relate to the services delivered to users and customers while, internally within IT, those services will be viewed as a number of components. Individuals or teams responsible for the running of particular components may not understand how their components fit into the overall delivery of a particular service. If an organisation is too externally focused, there is the risk that agreements will be made with the business that cannot be actually delivered due to a lack of understanding of how the internal constituent parts need to operate. Conversely, an organisation that is too internally focused is likely to struggle to understand and deliver business requirements.

- **Stability versus responsiveness:** Changes are frequently the causes of incidents and loss of availability, so it may be tempting to limit the number of changes in order to boost the stability of services. However, changes will always be needed in order to keep service up to date and to adopt to evolving business needs. The balance is between being able to speedily respond to changes and focusing on the stability of the infrastructure.

- **Quality of service versus cost of service:** There will always be pressures to boost the quality of IT services while controlling costs. Intense budgetary pressures may lead to reduced levels of service with more failures and less support. On the other hand, organisations out of balance on the 'other side' may be paying too much for their services with resilience built in that cannot be justified. The key is to have a meaningful dialogue over costs ensuring that the business fully understands what it gets and does not get for a certain amount of money and what it would get if it spent a little less or a little more.

- **Reactive versus proactive:** An extremely proactive organisation will always be predicting where things could go wrong and taking action to mitigate or prevent the situation. Taken to the extreme, such organisations may over monitor and apply unnecessary changes. Conversely, organisations that are purely reactive spend most of their time 'fire fighting' and dealing with situations as they arise, and they need to move more to the 'fire prevention' approach of predicting and avoiding incidents and problems.

## THE VALUE OF SERVICE OPERATION

Each of the stages of the ITIL service lifecycle adds and provides value to the business. Service operation does this by carrying out the processes and running the services as intended by the service strategy, service design and service transition stages of the lifecycle. Service operation is the visible face of the IT organisation and is the 'nearest' to the users and customers. Effective and efficient delivery of service is what is expected of service operation.

An underrated value of service operation is that it helps understand the effectiveness of the preceding lifecycle stages of service design and service transition. Many of the incidents that occur in service operation are the result of errors or omissions earlier in the service lifecycle.

## KEY ACTIVITIES AND FUNCTIONS

The processes performed by service operation are:

- **Event management:** This is the process responsible for the monitoring of all events throughout the IT infrastructure and applications to ensure normal operation. Event management is there to detect, interpret and alert in the event of a warning or exception event.

- **Incident management:** This is the process for dealing with all incidents. These may be incidents where service is being disrupted or where service has not yet been disrupted.

- **Request fulfilment:** This is the process that manages service requests and provides a channel for receiving them. Request fulfilment covers standard change requests, requests for information, and complaints and compliments. From a service desk perspective, the process of request fulfilment tends to cover all the calls that are neither incidents nor relate to problems.

- **Problem management:** This process is responsible for the management of all problems in the IT infrastructure. The process includes root cause analysis and arriving at the resolution of problems. Problem management remains responsible until resolutions are implemented typically via the processes of change management and release management.

- **Access management:** This process manages access rights to allow authorised users the right to access data, an application or service. It is also ensures that those without the required level of authorisation are not able to access data, applications and services.

The functions of service operation are:

- **The service desk:** This conducts a number of processes, in particular incident management and request fulfilment. The service desk is made up of a group of staff trained to deal with service events. Service desk staff will have access to the necessary tools to manage these events. The service desk ought to be the single point of contact for IT users within an organisation.

- **Technical management:** This is the function that provides the resources and ensures that knowledge of relevant technologies is kept up to date. Technical management covers all the teams or areas that support the delivery of technical knowledge and expertise. This includes teams such as networks, mainframe, middleware, desktop, server and database.

- **Application management:** This is the function that manages applications through the totality of their lifecycle. This starts with the first business 'idea' and completes when the application is taken out of service. Application management is involved in the design, testing and continual improvement of applications and the services that the applications support.

- **IT operations management:** This is responsible for operating the organisation's IT infrastructure and applications on a day-to-day basis. It includes such activities as event monitoring, printing, backups, scheduling and the management of the physical facilities such as the data centre, server room and back-up environment, including fire detection and suppression, temperature and humidity controls, and physical security controls.

The area which delivers the value has been modelled and designed elsewhere, so service operation will have many interfaces to processes that are part of the other lifestyle phases, in particular service asset and configuration management, release and deployment management, knowledge management, IT service continuity management and service level management.

## SELF-HELP

Organisations often utilise self-help offerings to enable users to resolve issues as they arise. The technology needs to be put in place to allow users to access information that will be helpful to them via a web-based front-end. Incident reporting and service requests can be handled in a similar fashion.

Self-help is cost-effective and aims to keep users active in their roles. Statistics can be gathered on the most frequently asked questions or most visited pages. This reduces the risk that training needs or technology gaps are not identified even though there has not been a logged service desk call.

Good communication is crucial for service operation. There needs to be active communication between IT teams and departments and with business areas and users. Members of staff undertaking service operation processes should be aware of the requirement to communicate on a regular basis with members of staff conducting other processes.

One should remember, however, that effective communication must have an understood purpose and, ideally, a specified audience. Too much communication without specific purpose or desired outcome can and usually will be counterproductive. Information overload tends to dull people's attention to new information and this can be just as bad as not communicating.

# 6 CONTINUAL SERVICE IMPROVEMENT

## INTRODUCTION

Once a service management solution has been implemented, it is essential not to sit back and think that the job has been done. All aspects of the environment will be continually changing and the service provider must always continue to seek improvements. Continual service improvement is responsible for ensuring that these improvements are identified and implemented. The performance of the IT service provider is continually measured and improvements are made to processes, IT services and the IT infrastructure in order to increase efficiency, effectiveness and cost-effectiveness.

## PURPOSE AND OBJECTIVES

### Purpose

Continual service improvement (CSI) aims to deliver business value by ensuring that the service management implementation continues to deliver the desired business benefits.

### Objectives

CSI has the following objectives:

- To review, analyse and make recommendations on where improvements could be made at any point throughout the lifecycle.
- To review and analyse service level achievements against targets.
- To identify and implement individual activities to improve service quality and the efficiency and effectiveness of service management processes.
- To improve the cost-effectiveness of delivering IT services without impacting customer satisfaction.
- To apply quality management methods to support continual improvement activities.

CSI must be an objective for everyone in the organisation, but improvement activities will only happen if they are properly managed. A senior responsible owner must be appointed and they must possess the appropriate authority to make things happen. This is not a trivial role, since improvements may mean significant disruption of current work patterns.

Improvement activities need to be planned and scheduled on an ongoing basis and their effects monitored to ensure that the desired improvement is achieved. Ideally, the culture of 'improvement' will become embedded within the organisation.

## Scope

CSI is applicable across all stages of the service lifecycle and addresses three main areas:

- The overall health of service management as a discipline.
- Continual alignment of the service portfolio with current and future business needs.
- The maturity of the enabling IT processes.

## Value to the business

CSI recognises that the value IT provides to the business can be realised and measured in different ways:

- **Improvements:** Outcomes that are better when compared with the previous state.
- **Benefits:** The gains achieved through the implemented improvements.
- **Return on investment (ROI):** The difference between the realised benefit and the cost of achieving it.
- **Value on investment (VOI):** The extra value created by the improvement including non-monetary benefits and outcomes.

Implementing CSI means committing to continued investment in order to create and maintain service improvement plans (SIPs).

The expected value from an investment is a critical component of any business case, and CSI stresses the need for periodic re-evaluation following the implementation of improvements by:

- checking that benefits/ROI/VOI are realised by specific improvements;
- identifying the best investments by estimating benefits from different initiatives;
- assessing the impact or current benefit of any proposed change of organisation structure or business strategy, or of regulatory or legislative change.

Many organisations have been traditionally very poor at checking that planned benefits have actually been delivered in the manner intended and hence often compound the situation by making future decisions on the assumption that some significant change in value has occurred.

## KEY PRINCIPLES

### Continual service improvement approach

The continual service improvement approach (see Figure 6.1) can be applied to any improvement plan. The approach consists of six steps:

**Figure 6.1 Continual service improvement approach**

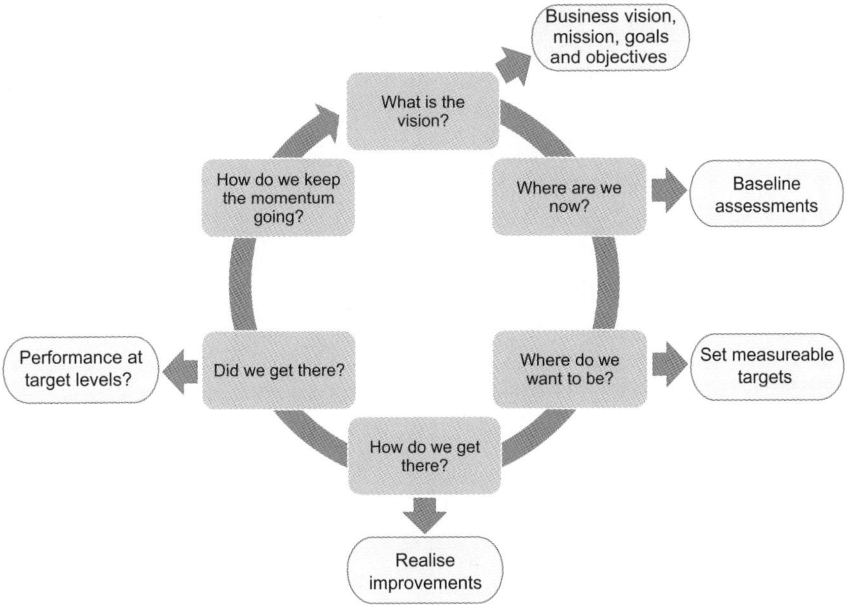

1. Clarify the vision, taking into account both the business and IT vision, mission, goal and objectives, and ensuring that everyone has a common understanding. Visions are aspirational and represent a desired state.
2. Assess the current situation and establish a baseline of exactly where the organisation is currently. This can be challenging and there is a need to be honest, which is why external input can be useful.
3. Define steps towards the vision based on priorities for improvement and setting measurable targets. It is usually impossible to leap from wherever you currently are direct to the state represented by the vision.
4. Document an improvement plan, using service and process improvement techniques.
5. Monitor achievements, making use of appropriate measures and metrics as defined earlier.
6. Maintain the momentum by ensuring that improvements are embedded and looking for further improvement opportunities.

## Delivering improvements

A CSI register should be kept to log the improvement opportunities and categorise them into small, medium and large. The expected time to implement each opportunity together with the anticipated and measureable benefits should also be indicated. Together, this information allows prioritisation of the improvement opportunities. The CSI register should be held as part of the service knowledge management system. The CSI register is the responsibility and accountability of the CSI manager.

A key to successful improvement is measurement. CSI advocates the use of industry approaches such as the Deming 'Plan–Do–Check–Act' model (see Chapter 34) and a process known as the 'seven-step improvement process' (see Chapter 32).

# SECTION 3:
# THE PROCESSES AND FUNCTIONS

# 7  BUSINESS RELATIONSHIP MANAGEMENT

## INTRODUCTION AND SCOPE

The long-term success of the IT service provider depends on its relationship with its customers. As in many other aspects of life, an effective long-term relationship requires commitment and effort on both sides in order to develop and maintain the trust and understanding that will underpin the relationship through good times and bad.

In its broadest sense the relationship between customer and IT service provider encompasses the full spectrum of business interactions between them, from operational matters concerned with service delivery and operational performance, through tactical issues, such as developing requirements or perhaps a business case for new or changed services, to the development of longer term strategy. Chapter 13 of this book describes how service level management (SLM) provides a platform for managing the relationship relative to operational and lower level tactical issues. This chapter describes how business relationship management (BRM) is used to align the activities of the service provider with the needs of its customer by developing, strengthening and maintaining the relationship for strategic and higher level tactical issues, and how BRM relates to other service management processes.

## PURPOSE AND OBJECTIVES

The primary purpose of BRM is to build and maintain an effective, productive relationship between customer and service provider, founded on an understanding of the customer and its business needs. This means more than reacting to new customer requirements. It is more profound than this. It is about understanding the customer, its strategy and business drivers sufficiently to be able to anticipate and influence the customer's requirements as circumstances change. Customer and provider have a common interest in ensuring that the customer understands the value of service offerings and has realistic expectations of them. For such a relationship to work there must clearly be commitment, trust, openness and honesty on both sides, and at times this will require the service provider to be open and honest about the customer, for example in relation to obligations the customer has failed to meet.

BRM must achieve a number of objectives if the relationship is to deliver. It must clearly be based on a sufficient understanding of the customer so that the service provider can develop its capabilities and resources in order to respond in an acceptable timeframe to the customer's changing needs and priorities, and, where relevant, to help the customer develop new requirements in response. The service provider will be able to anticipate, to an extent at least, how the customer's needs may change with circumstances, identifying how new or changed services or new technology offerings might help the customer respond effectively to change or improve performance. Close alignment between customer and service provider, and the insight this gives the service provider, will enable the service provider to identify real or potential conflicts between different parts of the customer's own organisation and help resolve or mitigate them. BRM places demands on both the service provider and the customer. BRM must continue to demonstrate the value of the relationship not only through meeting the objectives discussed above, but also by ensuring that the service provider meets its obligations for service performance and quality, achieving high levels of customer satisfaction in the process, among other things by providing an effective response to compliments and complaints.

## GENERAL PRINCIPLES

### The basis for BRM

The deployment of BRM is predicated on the argument that both service provider and customer will derive benefit from a relationship that seeks to align the activities of the service provider with the customer's developing business needs and improve the customer's understanding of the service provider's offerings and their value to the customer's business. This runs counter to the view that the supplier–customer relationship is fundamentally adversarial in nature. BRM requires commitment, so both sides should assess the value of BRM before deploying resources to it. A key issue for customers will be whether the business relationship is sufficiently important to make it worthwhile. The relationship between the customer and a provider of commodity services in a competitive marketplace will have less call for structured management than where the service is complex and of strategic importance to the customer. Service providers will similarly want to focus on major customers or customers that have strategic importance for them.

### Customer satisfaction

Customer satisfaction is a key concern for BRM because it is so for many other service management (SM) processes. However, customer satisfaction for BRM is less about delivering services to agreed targets for warranty and utility than about ensuring that the customer receives services that support its business objectives. The focus for BRM will be on the design and provision of services that add real value to the customer at a cost that is reasonable both in relationship to the value the services deliver and the costs of similar services from competitors.

### Business relationship management and service level management

The difference in focus between BRM and other processes is illustrated by the differences between BRM and service level management (SLM). Both processes are concerned with long-term relationships with the customer and with ensuring that the customer is happy with what is delivered. The focuses of SLM are on forging agreements with the customer on levels of service to be delivered for specific services and, by ensuring these service levels are met, on achieving acceptable levels of customer satisfaction. This means making sure that all SM processes, underpinning contracts and operational level agreements support the achievement of SLAs. BRM builds relationships with the customer that focus on strategic and higher level issues, seeking to provide services that are aligned to the business needs of the customer and are within the capability of the service provider to deliver. Customer satisfaction is a primary measure of the success of BRM, but this is customer satisfaction expressed in terms of the value of services to the customer.

### The customer portfolio

In order to be effective, BRM must maintain up-to-date information on its customers. It needs to understand who the customer really is, particularly in larger customer organisations where the real customers and decision makers may not be the same as the primary service users. In order to understand the value of services to the customer organisation and the impact of service changes, the service provider needs solid information on service users and on how the customer's business depends on the services that they receive. The provider needs information to assess the value of specific customers to its own business based on past and predicted usage and revenue streams. This will influence BRM decisions on the resources a provider will dedicate to BRM for specific customers. Knowledge of the customer's strategy and business plans enables BRM to position itself, in terms of resources and capabilities, to deal with changing customer demand. BRM should gather and maintain all this information in a customer portfolio, an information base that logically contains sufficient customer information to provide effective BRM.

### The customer agreement portfolio

Part of the information required on customers concerns the agreements between the service provider and the customer. This is a key source of information required by BRM and may be regarded logically as a component of the customer portfolio. In practice, however, it is best managed by service level management, which carries responsibility for negotiating and maintaining SLAs to ensure that all customer contracts and other agreements are managed centrally in order to make sure that the service provider does not undertake commitments it cannot meet. For internal service providers the agreements will be non-contractual, whereas for external service providers the agreements will be contractual. Depending on the nature and scale of the service provider, agreements may be standard agreements that are applied to all customers or agreements negotiated separately with each customer.

## KEY ACTIVITIES

The key activities of BRM are concerned with:

- understanding the customer and its business objectives and how these translate into service requirements;
- helping the customer formulate the requirements for new services and develop the customer's business case for investment in them;
- identifying changes that may affect the customers use of or requirements for services;

- identifying developments in technology and related matters that may provide opportunities for better services or lower costs for the customer;

- ensuring that the delivery and operation of services, including, for example, the transition into full operation, continues to recognise and satisfy the customer's business needs;

- measuring the level of customer satisfaction with the BRM process and the performance of the service provider as a whole;

- dealing with service reports, complaints, comments and other feedback to ensure the effective provision and continual improvement of delivered services.

## Other SM processes through the lifecycle

BRM by its very nature depends on and interacts with many of the other SM processes as it performs its various activities throughout the service lifecycle.

## RELATIONSHIPS WITH OTHER SERVICE MANAGEMENT PROCESSES

The importance to BRM of the customer portfolio and the customer agreement portfolio were discussed earlier in this chapter. In addition to these, BRM makes use of the following:

- **The IT service portfolio (see Chapter 10):** This is used by BRM to record information on new opportunities for BRM customers, as a source of information to help BRM evaluate new or changed services and to track progress and status of service developments for the customer.

- **The project portfolio:** This provides information in more detail on the status of projects planned or under way in relation to new or changed services for the customer.

- **The application portfolio:** This provides information on existing IT applications, the functionality they provide, the people who developed them and the people who support and manage them.

## Service portfolio management

BRM will work closely with service portfolio management, using information held in the service portfolio to identify the best way to exploit existing service offerings or capitalise on developments in the pipeline to meet customer needs. Where the existing service portfolio is unable to meet the needs of the customer, it will be necessary to develop a new service offering. BRM will work with the customer to articulate strategic requirements and desired outcomes, define patterns of business activity, identify stakeholders, develop the business case and ensure that adequate funding is available. It will work with service portfolio management internally to determine whether the service provider has the resources and capabilities to deliver.

## Availability, capacity, service level management and IT service continuity

BRM needs to work closely with service design teams to make sure that designed services continue to provide defined utility and warranty, working in collaboration with project teams to clarify or expand requirements and resolve conflicts. During this stage BRM will work with availability and capacity management to help them understand what the customer requires and why, continuing to work with the customer to develop and refine patterns of business activity and to articulate and agree requirements for disaster recovery/business continuity. Working alongside service level management, BRM will also be instrumental in the development of service level agreements and gaining the commitment of the customer to the SLM process. BRM has an important role to play in ensuring the customer's requirements for business continuity are properly understood and fed into IT Service Continuity Management.

## Change management, transition planning and support, knowledge management, and release and deployment management

BRM will ensure that change requests are submitted on behalf of the customer and that the customer's interests are fully represented in the change management process. BRM will also be involved in ensuring the customer is at a sufficient state of readiness to accept the new service, not only in terms of agreeing and validating user acceptance test plans and criteria and providing the resources required to conduct tests, but also in terms of making the necessary changes to processes and procedures through business change management. It will be involved with the customer in developing training and education plans, and including the customer in the development of knowledge management plans. BRM will also work with the customer in relation to release and deployment management to ensure that the customer understands the release and deployment plans, their impact on operations and the associated risks. BRM will need to confirm that there is adequate 'go live' and early life support in place, that training has been sufficient and fit for purpose and that the customer has full information on known errors and understands how these may affect the operation of the new service.

## Continual service improvement

Customer satisfaction measurement is a key activity for BRM throughout the lifecycle. Customer satisfaction measurement, service level management and the seven-step improvement process will all identify opportunities for service improvement, as will meetings between the customer and BRM to review service reports. Discussions at a more strategic level will identify areas where services need to be modified, replaced or terminated in response to external change drivers, such as new legislation and regulation, developing competition or varying economic conditions.

## Financial management for IT services

BRM helps financial management for IT services to understand how customers assess the value they get from IT services and what they are prepared to pay for them. BRM helps customers understand the IT service provider's financial policies, costs, risks and other issues, and clarifies how service provider costs translate into customer charges. Critically, BRM can help customers understand the financial implications of long-term planning decisions.

## METRICS

The performance of BRM is measured in relation to its key activities and the key performance indicators reflect this:

- Documented customer business objectives and desired business outcomes agreed with the customer and suitable for input into the service portfolio.
- Completed and signed-off requirements for new services and the customer's business case for their usage.
- Documented evidence of the identification of changes that may impact on delivered services and the service providers response to them.
- Opportunities to exploit new technology developments and other innovations are identified, assessed in collaboration with the customer, documented and recorded in the services portfolio.
- Documented evidence that delivered services effectively and efficiently meet the needs of the customer.
- Regular assessment of customer satisfaction demonstrating high levels of satisfaction, for example, through repeat business and positive recommendations to other potential customers.
- Documented evidence that continual service improvement is achieved in response to and through analysis of service reports, complaints, comments and other feedback.

## ROLES

The key roles in BRM, which may or may not be assigned to a single person, are the business relationship management process owner and the business relationship management process manager(s). The first of these is accountable for the proper performance of the BRM process in relation to its aims and the agreed policies and standards for its operation. The second of these two roles is concerned with the operational management of the BRM process. Whether it is appropriate for these two roles to be combined in a single person depends on the scale of the organisation and its structure in relation to other SM processes. Larger service provider organisations may have several business relationship managers, perhaps described as account managers, who will report to the BRM process manager and have responsibility for a single key customer or for a group of customers.

# 8 FINANCIAL MANAGEMENT FOR IT SERVICES

## INTRODUCTION AND SCOPE

No business can survive for long, let alone flourish, if it fails to manage its money effectively. Like any other business, the IT service provider, whether run as a commercial business or not, needs sound financial management. It must ensure it has the right amount of money available to put its plans into action, to make sure that it understands how its money has been used, to determine if the money has been used effectively or whether a proposed new investment is sound. It needs to understand what individual services cost to deliver and how these costs should be divided among the service users, so that, among other things, it can assess the impact of changes in demand and levy charges for service use if appropriate.

Financial management is about looking after the organisation's financial resources, making sure that they are prudently employed and that their use is properly accounted for. Financial management makes sure the organisation has an understanding of the costs of its operations, the structure of these costs and the things that influence them. It helps the organisation make the best decisions about the services it should provide, the way services should be provisioned, the investments required for their delivery and the effect of changing patterns of demand. It evaluates the value of services to the business and, if relevant, a basis for setting prices for them. Working with service portfolio management, it helps the organisation determine the services it should provide and those it should discontinue or change in some way.

Financial management helps with financial planning, making sure that the organisation's plans align with its ability to support the financial costs and manage the risks. It keeps track of expenditure so that it is clear how the money has been used. By routinely comparing expenditure and income with financial plans and budgets, financial management will identify potential problems and take appropriate action to keep the organisation on track. Where the IT service provider charges for service, financial management will advise on how this should be done and what charges should be levied.

IT service providers must work in a rapidly changing world. Businesses and the context in which they operate are constantly changing and the IT service provider must respond rapidly and effectively to these changes. Strong financial management enables the IT service provider to make better decisions and respond more rapidly to change. It enables better control over spending, ensures sound investment decisions and promotes value capture.

## PURPOSE AND OBJECTIVES

The aim of financial management for IT services is to ensure that optimal use is made of the organisation's financial resources and that this is achieved in compliance with the regulatory framework within which the IT service provider operates.

The purpose of financial management is to ensure that:

- money is managed and spent wisely;
- the financial resources available align fully with the organisation's plans and requirements for IT service delivery;
- investment decisions are sound and relevant to the organisation's objectives;
- financial risks are identified and managed effectively;
- governance arrangements are in place to ensure the effective stewardship of financial resources and to define clear accountabilities;
- the organisation complies with all relevant financial regulatory obligations and the overall financial policy and strategy of the business.

The key objectives are to ensure that:

- there is an effective system for financial planning and budgeting;
- financial plans and budget allocations are aligned with the service portfolio;
- all proposed investments have a business case that meets the standards of the organisation;
- all significant financial risks are identified and fully managed;
- there is an appropriate governance framework in place with clear accountabilities and all those who need to be are properly trained in relation to it;
- all financial expenditure is properly accounted for and there is an audit process to ensure proper stewardship of financial resources;
- the costs and value of all IT services, processes and activities are monitored, measured and understood and appropriate actions are taken on the basis of their financial performance.

## ACTIVITIES AND CONCEPTS

### Budgeting

It is important to plan ahead to make sure that business plans match the money available. The product of this planning is a financial plan or budget covering expected expenditure and income for a specified period, usually a (financial) year. Expenditure and income will be divided into categories to facilitate financial planning, management and control.

The budget must reflect the services to be delivered, new projects, investments and other planned changes. It is not an articulation of what the business hopes to do:

it is about what can be realistically achieved. Even so, a budget is a plan and plans do not always work out. Budgets should be the best prediction the organisation can make, but should include some contingency for the unexpected.

Budgets should show how expenditure and income are likely to change during the budget period (e.g. higher labour and transport costs at seasonally busy times).

Sound financial management requires regular monitoring against budgets. It tells the organisation when action is needed to maintain financial control, giving early warning that expenditure is too high or income too low; that planned projects cannot be funded or that others may be brought forward. Financial management may require managers to reduce expenditure or increase income to get back on track. Sometimes, variations in one part of the budget will be offset elsewhere and the budget can be revised accordingly. For example, lower expenditure on in-house employees offset by higher expenditure on contractors.

However, budgets must never be changed simply to bring them into line with the real world. Significant variations are a warning that things are not as expected. Good governance requires managers to take considered action in response.

## Accounting

The processes in IT accounting allow the IT service provider to account for expenditure and income, providing a breakdown of how costs and income are divided between customers, services and activities. This analysis helps determine the cost-effectiveness of services to make sound decisions about them. It provides details of how costs can be attributed to customers and customer groups, allowing the organisation to identify key customers and the impact of their service consumption. The information gathered through the accounting process provides budget monitoring with expenditure and income data, which will be used to evaluate the effectiveness of financial controls and to determine if action is required to rectify any significant variations from budget.

## Charging

The decision whether to charge is a strategic decision to be taken with due care. Charging not only increases the operating costs of the IT service provider, but also increases accountability, exposure and transparency. Customers can compare what they get from IT with what they have to pay and they can more easily compare their in-house IT provider with alternatives. Charging provides a means to influence customer behaviour, shaping demand and usage to match capacity, thereby reducing costs and risk. Without charging, many customers and users will see IT services as free and will make demands on these services with little interest in the financial or operational implications. The introduction of charging helps change attitudes.

## Service costing

An important aspect of good IT financial management is service costing. This means identifying the cost of providing each live service. Few organisations are currently able to do this, firstly because costs are typically not categorised in this way, but rather in terms of hardware, software, people, facilities etc. Secondly, organisations that haven't identified the services they provide, for instance in a service catalogue, cannot therefore attribute costs to those services. We believe that the IT industry is one of the few if not the only business sector that doesn't generally cost its services, but the value in doing so is significant. At the very least, service costing allows organisations to compare the relative value of different services, understand the cost benefit ratio of services, better decide when to retire a service and provide a greater degree of cost management. It also provides more meaningful information to the business about the cost of supporting business activities and processes and if service costs are defined in units the business understands, allows business users to understand and control their IT expenditure more effectively.

## Business case

All organisations need to invest wisely and a key role of financial management is to evaluate proposals for investment to determine whether they are worthwhile. Sound financial management will require all proposals for investment to include a clear case for making the investment. This case normally takes the form of a business case.

A business case is a decision support and planning tool that projects the likely consequences of a business action. The core of the business case is usually a financial analysis, but the justification of investments frequently depends on more than financial considerations.

---

**EXAMPLE**

A local authority wished to establish a service for quickly identifying whether a child had been previously identified as being at risk. If a child appeared at the local hospital accident and emergency department, the duty doctor would be able to check the child's details against the At Risk Register and notify Social Services if there was a positive result. This involved a considerable investment in IT systems and support services but there was no direct financial benefit. Nevertheless, the potential benefits (e.g. in avoiding the unnecessary death or injury of a child at risk) overrode the financial cost.

---

Financial management, in conjunction with business managers and other key stakeholders, will assess the business case in relation to the scale of the investment and the anticipated return, the impact on the business, the timescale for the realisation of benefits, the risks and contingencies involved, the robustness of the figures and their sensitivity to change. All of these should be covered in a sound business case.

It is essential that the business case makes it clear how the benefits and costs have been assessed, the assumptions on which it relies and the level of confidence in the figures. Business cases sometimes depend on highly optimistic or even dubious views of the future and it is crucial that this is made clear to the decision-makers. For example, it is common for business cases to predict staff savings based on individuals saving a few minutes of their time each day through a new investment. All these free minutes are aggregated, costed and presented as a benefit, even though there may be no practical way of realising a financial saving. It will also evaluate the resource requirements and take a view on whether the organisation has the resources and capabilities to deliver. An important concept is that of affordability. An investment may offer outstanding prospects, but the organisation should not give approval unless it can afford it.

## RELATIONSHIPS WITH OTHER SERVICE MANAGEMENT PROCESSES

Financial management for IT services is central to IT service management and it has links with many of the other service management disciplines. The key interactions are with service level management, service portfolio management, capacity management and service asset and configuration management.

### Service level management

Service level management (SLM) needs to work with financial management in relation to the costs of proposed levels of service required to meet the organisation's current and planned business needs. These costs will feed into the debate about what is affordable and deliverable and, therefore, what can be agreed in service level agreements (SLAs). If charging is in place, financial management will be involved in determining charges, including the use of differential charging as part of demand management. Financial management will assist in costing changes and evaluating new investments required to meet business needs.

### Service portfolio management

Financial management is concerned with business case development, assessment of investment opportunities, evaluation of different service options, the evaluation of financial risks and the determination of service value. All these are central to decisions about what should be included in the service portfolio or removed from it. Financial management is able to contribute to decisions on how best to provision a given service, whether this should be through the in-house IT service provider or a third-party provider. Financial management is also responsible for ensuring that funding is available to support the delivery of the service portfolio and for ensuring budget allocations align with it.

### Capacity management

Both availability and capacity management are concerned with cost-effective delivery of services, and financial management can assist by providing costing information to enable assessment of the financial impact of desired levels of capacity and availability. Proposals to invest in new capacity or in increased resilience can be assessed by financial management before action is taken to purchase. Where charging is in place, capacity management will be able to provide information on resource usage that will help financial management determine charges.

### Service asset and configuration management

Service asset and configuration management manages and maintains the configuration management database (CMDB), which holds financial and other information on assets that are required by financial management for a variety of uses. For example, from the CMDB, it should be possible to identify all the components required to deliver a given service and this information is used by financial management to determine the overall cost of the service. The CMDB also holds information on assets, such as equipment replacement dates and licence termination/renewal dates, which can be used in budget development and longer-term financial planning.

## Business relationship management

BRM helps financial management for IT services to understand how customers assess the value they get from IT services and what they are prepared to pay for them. BRM helps customers understand the IT service provider's financial policies, costs, risks and other issues, and clarifies how service provider costs translate into customer charges. Critically, BRM can help customers understand the financial implications of long-term planning decisions.

# 9 DEMAND MANAGEMENT

## INTRODUCTION AND SCOPE

Effective demand management avoids unnecessary spend on capacity and reductions in service levels caused by fluctuations in workload or demand.

As a service provider, IT is responsible for providing just enough capacity for services to meet their agreed service levels. Too much capacity is a wasted cost and too little puts service levels at risk. This is described in detail in the capacity management process (see Chapter 15).

The process of demand management is necessary for two main reasons:

- The arrival rate of work, such as transactions sent to a server, print jobs sent to a printer or calls to a service desk, is not steady. In other words, there are peaks and troughs over the hour and day, as well as seasonal increases or decreases in demand. There is rarely sufficient flexibility in IT resources to provide just enough capacity to meet the demand at each and every point in time.

- Fluctuations in demand and the challenge of providing just the right amount of capacity are sources of risk that the service provider should minimise. The decision on how much risk is acceptable is taken by the business, which may accept a level of spare capacity (and therefore extra cost) to reduce the risk.

In service management terms, 'demand' refers to the source of the work, such as the submission by the business/customers of batch jobs or a web search. It also refers to the activity that is subsequently generated on IT resources, such as network traffic and read/write calls to storage devices.

## PURPOSE AND OBJECTIVES

The purpose of demand management is to optimise the use of capacity by moving workload to less utilised times and resources. In so doing, more efficient use is made of the resources because their utilisation can be evened out over time instead of having to cater for peaks or troughs in load.

Demand management therefore requires to understand and influence customer demand for services in order to support the provision and management of minimum capacity to meet these demands.

The objectives include:

- characterising and codifying business activities into specific and recognisable patterns that have a common service consumption profile;
- characterising the usage of services by users into user profiles;
- encouraging the use of services at less busy times, for example by offering discounts at these times.

The first two objectives help to understand and predict the demand for resources better. This makes it easier for the service provider to match the services and resources to the identified needs of each user profile. Ultimately, this leads to improved value for both customers and suppliers by minimising costs and poor performance.

## UNDERSTANDING DEMAND FLUCTUATIONS

Since the work that creates the demand comes from the business, to understand how demand fluctuates we identify patterns of business activity. There is clearly a relationship between business activities and the consumption of IT resources. Our challenge is to understand that relationship well enough so that when the business shares its plans and forecasts with us, we can predict the impact on our resources. This in turn will tell us which resources need to be replaced or upgraded and when, so that we can cost-effectively plan and budget our IT spend.

## ATTEMPTING TO REDUCE PEAK DEMANDS

Provided the business agrees, IT can look to influence demand to reduce peak workloads and protect service levels without spending money on capacity that would otherwise be unused most of the time. Consider Figure 9.1 that shows a workload profile of demand over a twelve-month period.

In this scenario, IT has to provide capacity for 165 units of work in July and 172 in August. However, without this two-month peak, a capacity to handle only 130 units of work is necessary. Therefore, if IT can smooth out this peak demand and spread the workload in July and August across other months, it could potentially save the cost of providing capacity for up to 42 extra units of work.

One way of limiting demand is to increase the price for work units at peak times and/or reduce the price at off-peak times. Another way is to restrict the workload, for example in an online application by limiting the number of concurrent users, or in a service desk by reducing the number of lines available to callers.

## PATTERNS OF BUSINESS ACTIVITY

Patterns of business activity (PBAs) can often be conveniently associated with a small number of defined user profiles. In this way we can relate any new individual, team or department to a particular user profile to understand their impact on resources rather than spending the effort to consider them individually.

**Figure 9.1 Workload profile**

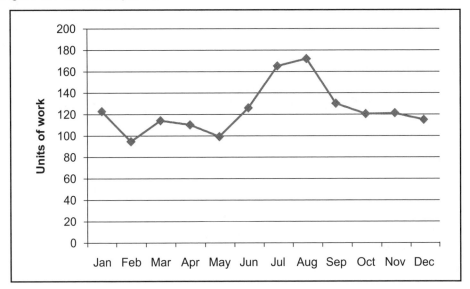

## USER PROFILES

User profiles should be based on the roles and responsibilities in an organisation. In this way, each user profile can be assigned to one or more PBA. Applications and processes can also be profiled in the same way as users. This approach allows patterns and profiles to be matched in order to understand and manage customer demand more easily and accurately.

## THE BENEFITS OF DEMAND MANAGEMENT

Once the demand management process has understood demand fluctuations and applied controls to limit peak demand, capacity management becomes more effective in planning capacity, reducing unnecessary spend and acquiring resources more cost-effectively. As a result, service levels improve and the business gains increased confidence in IT's ability to meet both its present and future requirements.

## RELATIONSHIPS WITH OTHER SERVICE MANAGEMENT PROCESSES

### Capacity management

Demand management is a key contributor to capacity management because it helps understand the nature of demand on resources and can reduce the capacity requirements by smoothing out peaks in demand.

**Service portfolio management, service catalogue management**

Codifying patterns of business demand and user profiles can contribute to service portfolio and service catalogue management by helping to align services to particular business needs and requirements.

**Financial management**

Financial management can contribute to demand management by assisting with financial uplifts and discounts to influence and smooth demand across peaks and troughs.

## METRICS

There are no standard metrics associated with this process, but we offer some suggestions below:

- The peak: average load ratio (should reduce over time with effective demand management).
- The percentage of users who have been profiled.
- For a given period (e.g. one year) the amount of spend avoided through demand management.
- The percentage of services in the service catalogue that have been validated against user profiles and PBAs.

## ROLES

Only large IT operations are likely to have a demand manager. It is more likely that the demand management activity will be undertaken by the capacity manager.

# 10 SERVICE PORTFOLIO MANAGEMENT

## INTRODUCTION AND SCOPE

The service portfolio, which gives a management-level view of all IT services as they move through the service lifecycle, is a critical management system in service management. It has three parts:

- The service pipeline that holds information on services that are under development.

- The service catalogue that holds details of all services either already in production or ready to move into production.

- Retired services that have been discontinued from operational use.

The service portfolio therefore provides a complete picture of all services under development for future delivery, services in production and services that have come to the end of their productive life. It is the foundation for managing the full lifecycle for all services in terms of their business requirements, the business case for investment, the financial and other resources required for service development and operation, the risks associated with the development and operation of the service and, where relevant, how the service will be priced.

The IT service provider, in conjunction with the business, will identify a number of opportunities for investment in new or changed IT services. Before any of these opportunities are transformed into a service, important decisions must be made about the value of the new services to the business, the capacity of the IT service provider and the marketplace to deliver the service, and the relative priority of the proposed service in comparison with other potential investments. In other words, the organisation will need answers to questions such as:

- Why should we invest in this service rather than something else?

- What value will it deliver to the business?

- What will it cost to deliver the service solution and can we afford it?

- Do we have the resources and capabilities to deliver it?

- How does this investment fit with our broader strategy?

- What are the dependencies with other investments in progress or under consideration?

- What are the risks?

- Is the return on the investment acceptable in terms of investment cost, risks and timescale?

## PURPOSE AND OBJECTIVES

The purpose of service portfolio management (SPM) is to ensure that decisions to invest in IT services are sound and are fully aligned with the needs and priorities of the business. Once a decision is made to invest, the investment must be managed through its lifecycle. SPM's goal here is to ensure that the investment delivers optimum value to the organisation. As a management support system, the service portfolio enables the organisation to answer strategic questions about its services, customers and pricing, as well as helping it set priorities and plan resource allocation.

An objective of SPM is to ensure there is an effective methodology for the evaluation of potential investments. Once an investment has been agreed, the purpose of SPM is to ensure that the investment is managed effectively throughout its lifecycle. Among other things this is about ensuring proper governance arrangements are in place, that investments and their business case are reassessed against changing conditions both within and outside the organisation and that the realisation of benefits is properly managed.

The objectives of SPM are:

- to develop and maintain a service portfolio that provides a complete picture of all services including their status;

- to establish conditions and requirements for inclusion of new services in the service portfolio;

- to ensure a service catalogue is developed and managed as part of the portfolio, and agree the rules for transferring services to the service catalogue as they move into transition and out of the catalogue and as they move into retirement;

- to ensure the service portfolio meets the functional and performance requirements of its users and that its performance, availability and security meet agreed requirements;

- to ensure that management reports are produced in line with agreed reporting requirements.

## SERVICE PORTFOLIO COMPONENTS

The service portfolio contains information about services across the entire lifecycle, providing information on the status of services as they move from concept through requirement specification, approval, design, transition into live operation and eventual retirement. The information held on each service develops and changes as it moves through the lifecycle. In the early part of the lifecycle, there will be little more than a description of the proposed service with details of the value proposition, business sponsors and other basic details. As we move through the lifecycle, requirements will be specified and either incorporated or cross-referenced. The business case will be included along with funding details, priorities and risks. Offerings and packages, costs and prices will be added once designed and agreed.

By the time the service is ready for operational delivery, the full content of the service portfolio should include:

- service name;
- service description;
- service status;
- service classification and criticality;
- applications used;
- data and/or data schema used;
- business processes supported;
- business owners;
- business users;
- IT owners;
- service warranty level, SLA and SLR references;
- supporting services;
- supporting resources;
- dependent services;
- supporting OLAs, contracts and agreements;
- service costs;
- service charges (if applicable);
- service revenue (if applicable);
- service metrics.

In order to manage and understand the information, the service portfolio is separated conceptually, and often physically, into three separate components: the service pipeline, the service catalogue and retired services. These are described in more detail below.

The structure of the service portfolio and its relationship with systems and areas are illustrated in Figure 10.1.

From a broader perspective, the service portfolio is best included as a part of the IT service provider's service knowledge management system.

## Figure 10.1  The service portfolio

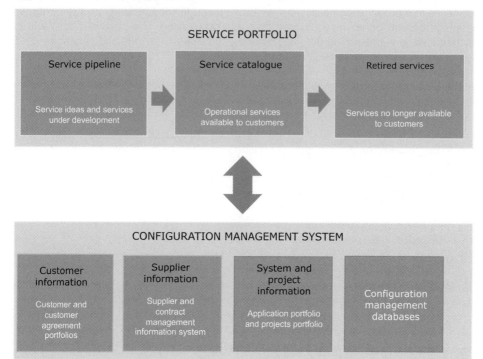

## The service pipeline

The service pipeline holds details of all services that are not yet ready for transition into production. It gives IT service provider management a complete view of their plans for new and changing services, and it is a measure of the IT provider's vision for, and confidence in, the future. It reflects the IT provider's service strategy.

## The service catalogue

The service catalogue contains information about IT services that are currently in production or are about to go through service transition into production. It is therefore a measure of the IT service provider's current capacity, capability and confidence to deliver. The service catalogue is the part of the service portfolio that is available to customers and is written in language suitable for this purpose.

## Retired services

Services eventually come to the end of their useful life, perhaps because they are no longer relevant to the customer's needs or because they are no longer cost-effective. There is no point continuing with a service that is not wanted or is uneconomical to run, unless there is an alternative justification for its retention.

Information about retired services should be retained as part of the IT service provider's service knowledge management system for as long as such information is likely to be useful. In some circumstances, a retired service may become operationally viable and be taken out of retirement.

## KEY ACTIVITIES

Service portfolio management is about how decisions are made to include new services and the continual review of existing services in the service portfolio. This is best described as a cyclic process that moves around the Define–Analyse–Approve–Charter loop illustrated in Figure 10.2.

**Figure 10.2  The service portfolio management cycle**

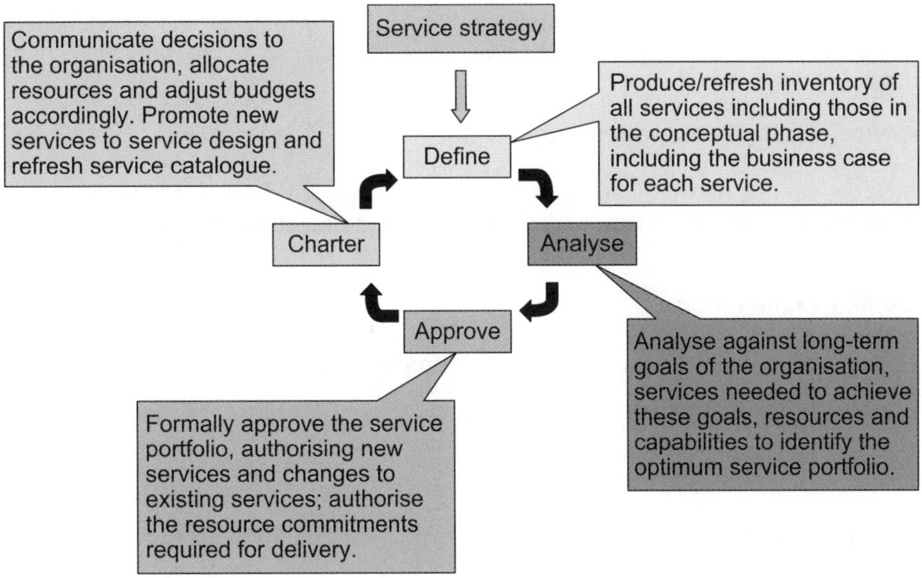

## RENEWING THE PORTFOLIO

As circumstances change (e.g. changes in the economic outlook, changes in raw material prices or labour costs, marketplace changes etc.) decisions made on the content of the service portfolio will need to be reassessed. Part of service portfolio management must therefore involve monitoring the commercial, social, economic and political environment to identify events that should trigger a reassessment of the service portfolio.

## RELATIONSHIPS WITH OTHER SERVICE MANAGEMENT PROCESSES

Its importance throughout the lifecycle and its value to all other processes and functions, means that the service portfolio is described as the 'spine' that links the different lifecycle stages together.

## Business relationship management

Service portfolio management is a critical management system supporting the way the IT service provider works in conjunction with the business to ensure that IT adds optimum value. Managing the service portfolio requires full collaboration with the business and this means involvement from business relationship management.

## Financial management

One of the key relationships for service portfolio management is with financial management. The contribution from financial management is concerned with business case development, assessment of investment opportunities, comparative evaluation of different service options, the evaluation of financial risks and the determination of service value. All these are central to decisions about what should be included in the service portfolio or removed from it.

Financial management is also responsible for ensuring that funding is available to support the delivery of the service portfolio and for ensuring budget allocations align with it.

## Service catalogue management

Since the service portfolio includes the service catalogue there needs to be a close relationship between service portfolio management and service catalogue management. The information in both elements of the service portfolio must be consistent.

## Supplier management

Supplier management ensures that all supporting services and their details and relationships are accurately reflected within the service portfolio and that the service portfolio is consistent with the supplier and contract management information system. Supplier management will draw on information in the service portfolio as a basis for negotiating underpinning contracts.

## Other processes

The service level management process depends heavily on the content and quality of the service portfolio, especially the service catalogue.

Capacity management has an input into the service portfolio to ensure that new technologies are given due consideration in service planning. The service portfolio is a key input to capacity management.

The construction and maintenance of the service portfolio requires input from IT operations management and technical and applications management to ensure the service portfolio is accurate and achievable.

# 11 DESIGN COORDINATION

## INTRODUCTION AND SCOPE

The design coordination process ensures that all design activities associated with both new and changed services are understood and coordinated. This includes the design work included in changes, projects and support work as well as supplier activity.

Design coordination is responsible for making sure that the design of services and their supporting infrastructure are consistent and in line with the present business requirements as well as taking into account emerging requirements.

The design coordination process is a key part of the service design stage of the service lifecycle and highlights the need to coordinate, control and monitor the various activities undertaken within service design. This coordination, control and monitoring ensures consistency is achieved. Without design coordination, there is a risk that service design activities become inconsistent and do not contribute to the realisation of the business requirements.

## PURPOSE AND OBJECTIVES

It is the purpose of design coordination to ensure that all design activities are consistent and coordinated. This includes the design work included in changes, projects and support work as well as supplier activity. The scope of design coordination is all service design activity.

Objectives include coordinating the design of services, processes, technology and architecture as well as service management metrics and information gathering systems.

In addition, design coordination has the objectives of:

- planning and coordinating the necessary resources and capabilities;
- producing the service design package;
- managing quality criteria;
- ensuring that service models and solutions confirm to strategic, architectural and governance requirements.

Simply put, design coordination brings governance and control to the various activities of service design.

## BASIC CONCEPTS

There are many activities often running in parallel that make up service design. Some of these activities are high profile, some less so. There is a risk that some service design activities operate in a vacuum separated from other design activity and the ongoing operational management of existing services.

Design coordination must ensure that all design activity is understood and controlled with information about revised requirements or changes in the operating environment communicated. Design coordination takes the holistic or macro view across design activity leaving the individual design teams to concentrate on the micro activity.

## ACTIVITIES

The key activities of design coordination are:

- production and maintenance of design standards, policies and guidelines to cover all service design activities and processes;
- governance and monitoring to ensure that the relevant business requirements are recognised and incorporated in service design activities;
- prediction and utilisation planning of the capabilities and resources required for service design activities;
- coordinating the resources, activities and processes within the service design stage of the service lifecycle;
- tracking the capability and resource utilisation against plan throughout the Service Design activities;
- management of design issues and risks;
- close liaison with project areas and change designers throughout the service design activities in order to ensure consistency;
- producing (or ensuring the production of) the service design package;
- improving the efficiency and effectiveness of the design stage of the service lifecycle.

## CHALLENGES

Care needs to be taken in order to ensure that design coordination retains its high-level view of design activity and does not get too involved in the lower level design work.

There is also a risk that design coordination is not seen as having sufficient authority within the organisation to enforce the usage of its guidelines, standards and policies.

This may particularly be the case when dealing with high-profile, large projects that are budget and resource rich. Design coordination must ensure that its role in ensuring consistency of design is fully understood and communicated.

## RELATIONSHIPS WITH OTHER SERVICE MANAGEMENT PROCESSES

Design coordination pulls together the activities that take place in service design. It performs a similar role to that undertaken by transition planning and support within the service transition phase of the service lifecycle.

There is also a strong link to project management activity. Design coordination is in a position to provide projects with guidelines, standards and policies in relation to the design of services and then to monitor adherence to these guidelines, standards and policies throughout the life of the project. Design coordination helps to ensure that the project deliverables are what are required and expected and that all areas are working in the same direction.

## METRICS

Metrics in the design coordination sphere will centre on the degree of conformance to policies and standards throughout the service design activities.

## ROLES

The key role is that of design coordinator. It is the design coordinator who is responsible for ensuring that the activities of design coordination take place and that all design activity is monitored and controlled.

# 12  SERVICE CATALOGUE MANAGEMENT

## INTRODUCTION AND SCOPE

Service catalogue management provides a basis for customer-focused management of IT service delivery, which helps ensure that IT service offerings are aligned with the needs of the business. It does this by providing clear and consistent information on services in a language that the customers will understand and in a format that customers will want to use, thus enabling a constructive dialogue about IT services where all parties have a common understanding of what is being discussed. In this way the process of ordering standard services is simplified and made more efficient because what is being offered is clear, the terms and conditions for its provision are clear and there is a simple and consistent self-service mechanism in place for obtaining it.

Service catalogue management, through the production and maintenance of the technical service catalogue, provides a source of technical information that enables the IT service provider to manage services more effectively.

Information in the service catalogue enables a better understanding of how the delivery of IT services impacts the business as well as the risks and vulnerabilities that require to be managed by the IT service provider. This provides service level management with a source of information for reporting to customers on performance, costs and other service issues and provides supplier management with a sound basis for contract negotiation with suppliers.

Integrating the service catalogue with the configuration management database (CMDB) provides a mechanism for linking the outward-looking, business-focused aspects of service provision with the internal, technically focused aspects of service management.

The provision and management of the service catalogue is in itself a service delivered by the IT service provider. As such it should encompass all the elements of a service including any SLAs between IT and the customers who use it.

In broad terms, service catalogue management has two elements:

- The initial design and development of the service catalogue: its content and structure, its relationship with the remainder of the service portfolio, in particular the transfer of services from the service pipeline, the relationship with the configuration management database, the processes, accountabilities and responsibilities for keeping it up to date, audit, etc.

- The ongoing management of the service catalogue: managing the information in the service catalogue to keep it up to date, complete and accurate as the business and technical environment change, coordinating with changes to the rest of service portfolio and the configuration management database, managing availability, security and performance.

## PURPOSE AND OBJECTIVES

Keeping the service catalogue up to date, accurate and complete does not happen by accident. It needs to be managed. In ITIL, the aim of the service catalogue management process is to ensure that an up-to-date service catalogue is developed and maintained.

The purpose of service catalogue management is to create and maintain a service catalogue of all services currently delivered or ready to be delivered by the IT service provider. Service catalogue management must ensure that the service catalogue meets the agreed functionality, usability, accessibility, availability and performance requirements of all those who need to use it.

The objectives of service catalogue management are:

- to manage the information in the service catalogue, ensuring its accuracy in terms of the characteristics of live services and those being prepared for live operation in accordance with defined policies;
- to ensure that the service catalogue can be appropriately accessed by authorised users;
- to ensure that service dependencies and interfaces are accurate and support the use of the service catalogue by other service management processes.

## KEY ACTIVITIES

### Service catalogue design

The service catalogue, a key part of the service portfolio, is a central source of information about the services delivered or about to be delivered by the IT service provider.

The service catalogue is a subset of the service portfolio, the contents of which are described in Chapter 10. However, because it is customer facing, the service catalogue must include information that is important and of direct interest to the customer. This will include information such as:

- details of service and product offerings;
- service availability;
- support services;
- support arrangements;
- key policies;
- terms and conditions;

- service level agreements;
- charges and prices;
- ordering and cancellation;
- key future plans (e.g. where there are existing plans to phase out, replace or change a service).

The service catalogue as a whole serves two purposes. First, it provides information on services to the customers of the IT service provider in a way that enables the customer to understand and make decisions about the services it uses or might wish to use. Second, it is a primary source of information for the IT service provider on the services it offers to its customers.

In many organisations, this dual purpose is reflected in the structure of the service catalogue, which is divided into two main parts: a business service catalogue, which describes services in terms that are helpful and useful to the business, and a technical service catalogue, which describes services in terms that are useful and helpful to the IT side.

Leading practice is for the source information about customer services, supporting services and the relationships to business processes and IT components to be held in a single location as part of the configuration management system. The service catalogue can then be presented to readers in one of a number of 'views' according to their perspective. Two such views are usually referred to as the 'business' or 'customer' service catalogue view and the 'technical' or 'supporting' service catalogue view. For the remainder of this chapter, these two views will be referred to as the 'business service catalogue' and the 'technical service catalogue'.

## The business service catalogue

As a primary vehicle for communications between the IT service provider and its customers, the business service catalogue should be as easy to use as any good mail order catalogue. The business service catalogue will serve its purpose best if it meets its users' requirements. This means engaging with the user community in requirement gathering and design. If the business service catalogue does meet the customers' needs, they will be unlikely to use it. Among other things, it is important that there is a common understanding of what the word 'service' means.

What is often a source of confusion is that what the customer sees as a single service is most likely to be seen by the IT service provider as a mix of services, with a core service underpinned by supporting services (see Figure 12.1).

**EXAMPLE**

The Payroll service, which the customer regards as a single service, relies on a whole host of supporting services such as PC support and server support, the network infrastructure, the corporate email service, to name but a few. Then there are printing services, security services and accommodation services. Payslips, sorted into mail-sort or walk-sort sequence, may be transported from the data centre's print facility to the finance department by an internal courier service.

**Figure 12.1 The difference between core and enhancing or supporting services**

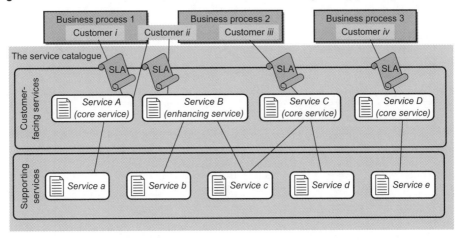

The actual information included in the business service catalogue will vary from organisation to organisation, but most will contain information similar to that shown in Figure 12.2.

The design of the business service catalogue is always a balance between too much and too little information. There is sometimes a tendency to include information because it might be useful. The key point is to remember for whom it is intended. Some customers may have the time to plough through hundreds of pages of fine detail, but most will have neither the time nor the inclination to do so. The answer is to be brief and to the point, avoid jargon and acronyms and aim for ease of comprehension rather than trying to impress the customer with technical brilliance.

## The technical service catalogue

This part of the service catalogue holds details of services from an IT perspective, including a service description in IT terms along with details of the key components or configuration items (CIs) that make up the service and the relationship between them. It describes in technical terms the supporting services listed in the business service catalogue and explains the interrelationships and interdependencies between them. It should also include, if only by cross reference, details of relevant operational level agreements (OLAs) and underpinning contracts (UCs). It will ideally include information on key personnel who are either responsible for or provide some kind of technical authority in respect of the service. The technical service catalogue is neither intended for nor usually made available to customers.

As with the business service catalogue, it is easy to put too much detail into the technical service catalogue. The important point in its design is to have a clear understanding of how the technical service catalogue will be put to use, remembering that more information generally means a higher maintenance and management cost. Listing all the technical staff who support a service might have some use, but people come and go, change roles, get promoted and so on, and this kind of detail easily gets out of date.

**Figure 12.2  Example business service catalogue**

| Service name: | | | Service: S001 ref | | S002 | S003 | S004 |
|---|---|---|---|---|---|---|---|
| Short description: Cross reference to detailed description ⇨ | | | Service: type | | | | |
| Manager responsible: Contact details: | Support contact: Contact details: | | Business owner: Contact details: | | | | |
| Service ordering details: Link to online order form (if applicable) ⇨ | | | | | | | |
| Service charges/tariff (if applicable): | | | | | | | |
| Business unit #1 using service: | Business owner: | Contact details: | Business impact and priority: | SLA ref: | | | |
| Business unit #2 using service: | Business owner: | Contact details: | Business impact and priority: | SLA ref: | | | |
| Business unit #3 using service: | Business owner: | Contact details: | Business impact and priority: | SLA ref: | | | |
| Supporting service: #1 | Name and brief description | | | Catalogue cross ref ⇨ | | | |
| Supporting service: #2 | Name and brief description | | | Catalogue cross ref ⇨ | | | |
| Supporting service: #3 etc | Name and brief description | | | Catalogue cross ref ⇨ | | | |
| Customer requirements: e.g. information input; desktop hardware and operating software; | | | | | | | |
| Standard, optional and excluded items; | | | | | | | |
| Performance: service hours; key performance targets; business continuity arrangements; etc. | | | | | | | |
| Special conditions: e.g. security (link to security policy ⇨) | | | | | | | |

# RELATIONSHIPS WITH OTHER SERVICE MANAGEMENT PROCESSES

## Service portfolio management

The service catalogue is part of the service portfolio that contains information about services that are currently delivered by the IT service provider or are ready to move into transition to live operation. In other words, they are services at the stage in their service lifecycle where they will be of direct interest to customers.

Service catalogue management and service portfolio management must work together to agree when and how services in the service pipeline will transfer into the service catalogue. This requires monitoring the status of the service through service design to be ready to update the service catalogue when the service is ready for transition to live operation. There will be similar considerations when the service is ready to be retired from live operation.

## Service asset and configuration management

In organisations with a comprehensive configuration management database (CMDB), all parts of the service catalogue should be an integrated part of the CMDB, which would otherwise hold duplicate information on CIs and relationships already in the service catalogue. If services are each defined as a CI, as part of a hierarchy of services, it is possible to relate incidents and changes to services affected. It also provides information to capacity and availability management and assists service continuity management perform business impact analysis. It also provides a basis for service monitoring and reporting.

In organisations without a complete CMDB, the production of the service catalogue can be a good starting point for its development.

## Financial management

The service catalogue provides financial management with the information required on service demand for modelling, decision-making and control. It not only enables improved budgeting and planning, but also supports comparative benchmarking against other providers.

It must be remembered that customers expect that all services in the business service catalogue are available for use and so, as soon as a service has moved into the service catalogue, it must be made available to customers who demand it. Due diligence is necessary to ensure that the service is a complete product that can be fully supported. This includes technical feasibility, financial viability and operational capability. Financial management has a clear role in this activity.

## Business relationship management

The business relationship management process defines the service-to-customer relationships and how the service meets customer needs.

## Service level management

Service level management provides details of service warranty levels for inclusion in the service catalogue.

## ROLES

The service catalogue manager's responsibilities include ensuring that:

- all services in operation and new services moving into transition are correctly recorded in the service catalogue;
- retired services are removed from the service catalogue at the appropriate time;
- the service catalogue is maintained to be accurate, complete and up to date;
- the service catalogue continues to serve the needs of those who need to use it.

# 13 SERVICE LEVEL MANAGEMENT

**INTRODUCTION AND SCOPE**

Service level management (SLM) exists to ensure that services fully align with the needs of the business and meet the customers' requirements for functionality, availability and performance. The aim is to ensure that levels of service are negotiated and agreed with customers and all services are delivered to the agreed service levels defined in terms of agreed performance indicators. SLM must also ensure that services are continually improved where improvements are required by the customer and can be justified in terms of their cost.

SLM is the steward of the relationship between the IT service provider and its customers and is accountable to the user for the services delivered.

The principal activities of SLM are:

- to develop and negotiate SLAs with customers;
- to ensure SLAs are underpinned by internal (OLAs) and external (UCs) agreements that support the achievement of agreed service levels;
- to act as a bridge between the IT service provider and the business;
- to manage and maintain positive, constructive relationships with the customer. As the primary interface between IT and the business, it must be kept up to date with all relevant developments.

SLM helps IT become more professional, consistent and productive in its relationship with customers, creating and keeping open effective lines of communication. It ensures IT focuses on what matters most to the customer and the business and helps IT to deliver better value for money.

It ensures services are aligned to the needs of the business, providing a clear basis for the delivery of services including the definition of roles and responsibilities for both sides, provides measurable and achievable targets for service delivery, helps build a better mutual understanding and helps improve customer satisfaction with IT services.

**PURPOSE AND OBJECTIVES**

Service level management exists to ensure that services fully align with the needs of the business and meet the customers' requirements for functionality, availability and performance. The aim is to ensure that levels of service are negotiated and agreed with customers and all services are delivered to the agreed service levels defined in terms of agreed performance indicators. SLM must also ensure that services are continually improved where improvements are required by the customer and can be justified in terms of their cost.

SLM is vital to continual service improvement (CSI). SLM's objective is to maintain and improve IT service quality by a continuing process of agreeing, monitoring and reporting on IT service achievements and initiating corrective action where there is a business case for doing so and the business agrees that action should be taken. SLM supports the seven-step improvement process because SLM determines what is to be measured, monitored and reported. It works with the business and customers to agree new requirements and identify service improvement opportunities and priorities. This information and the activities it drives are an important part of CSI.

The purpose of the SLM process is to ensure that all delivered services are monitored and measured against the agreed levels of service and that the results, expressed in accordance with the customers' needs, are reported regularly to the business and customers.

The objectives of SLM are:

- to build and maintain effective, productive relationships with customers;
- to define and agree with customers the required levels of IT services in a way that customers understand;
- to manage the performance of services to ensure agreed levels are achieved and that customers are happy with what they receive;
- to ensure systems are in place continually to improve service levels if the organisation wants it and the cost is justified and affordable.

## BASIC CONCEPTS

Service level management provides a bridge between the IT service provider and the business, operating as a focal point for customers and the business in their dealings with the IT service provider. Through regular contact and communication, SLM must represent the IT service provider to the business, and the business to the IT service provider. From its central position, SLM is able to build strong and effective relationships between the IT service provider and the business customers, managing their expectations and ensuring that delivered services meet or exceed those expectations.

### Service level requirements

The needs of the business, expressed in terms the business understands, are documented as service level requirements (SLRs), which contain a definition of the services the customers need, including key performance and availability targets. The SLRs will be translated by the IT service provider into service specifications, which define how the IT provider will make the services available, including the use of third-party providers.

## SERVICE LEVEL AGREEMENTS

Where one party delivers services to another, it is a good idea to have some kind of agreement setting out the basis on which the service is provided. Such agreements would normally contain, among other things, a description of what is to be provided, the key performance indicators, the way the service is to be charged (where relevant) and the responsibilities of each of the parties. In SLM, the agreements between the internal IT service provider and the business customers that it supports are known as service level agreements (SLAs) and it is through SLAs that SLM manages the relationship between itself and its customers.

### SERVICE LEVEL AGREEMENT

A service level agreement (SLA) is an agreement between an IT service provider and a customer that describes the IT service and service levels, and specifies the responsibilities of both parties.

In order to be effective, the SLA should be a written document signed off by all parties affected by it. SLAs are important so they will rarely be agreed without negotiation between the IT service provider and the customer, beginning with a statement of intent that sets out the terms, conditions and targets to be agreed. It has to be in a language that both sides will understand. This means in the language of the customer and not the technical language or jargon of the provider. The SLA defines (in language that has meaning to the customer) precisely what is to be delivered and when and where it is to be delivered. It also defines the standard of quality to be delivered, usually in terms of performance and availability. It will define the responsibilities of both the service provider and the customer. This is important. It makes little sense for a service provider to commit to deliver a service without making it clear what is expected of the customer.

The SLA will include contact details, what should happen if something goes wrong, the way any disputes should be handled, any provisions for redress, the mechanism for getting the SLA changed if necessary and the period over which the agreement will stand unless otherwise changed by agreement. If the service is to be chargeable, then the way charges are to be determined and the arrangements for invoicing should be included. Charges may also be included in a separate document, the tariff, referenced in the SLA.

It is common in IT for individual services to be shared by a number of customers, and individual customers will use a range of services. This means that there is a choice in designing SLAs: they can be customer-based, where an SLA covers a range of services delivered to a particular customer; or they can be service-based, where a common SLA covers all customers of a given service.

### Customer-based SLAs

A customer-based SLA is an agreement with a specific customer or customer group covering all the IT services they use. For example, a local authority education department might have a single agreement embracing payroll, school administration, human resources, purchasing, financial management systems and so on. In some ways, this simplifies the relationship between IT and the customer, putting the customer's perspective to the fore. On the other hand, customer-based SLAs are complex and often difficult to agree and manage. Additionally, customers may be disappointed that the same service levels available to them, for common services such as email, for example, cannot be tailored to their specific needs.

## Service-based SLAs

A service-based SLA is an agreement with all the customers of a specific service. An example might be the organisation's intranet service. This kind of agreement makes good sense where all customers are offered the same level of service, but becomes complicated when this is not the case. Sometimes, different levels of service are inevitable (e.g. where remote users have to rely on low-speed communications). Alternatively, customers may simply demand choice. For example, some organisations will offer a PC support service with identical terms and conditions for all users, but others may offer different levels of service according to what the customer is prepared to pay. Using banded levels of service (e.g. bronze, silver and gold support levels) is a very common way of simplifying this problem. Another issue with service-based SLAs is who signs on behalf of the customer and who represents them. Having user groups with elected representatives or spokespersons is one solution.

## Multi-level SLAs

Some organisations choose a multi-level SLA approach, where elements of services common to all customers are covered by a corporate-level SLA. Issues relating to a particular customer or customer group, no matter what the service, are then covered by a customer-level SLA and all issues relating to a specific service for the customer or customer group are covered by a service-specific SLA.

The SLA for a service must be based on realistic, achievable targets (e.g. for performance and availability). The achievement of these targets depends on the performance of the internal and external services that underpin the delivery of the main service. Putting it another way, SLAs must reflect the levels of service actually being delivered or that can be delivered. They are about what can be done rather than what we would like to be done. If a customer requires a different level of service, this would normally be dealt with by raising a service level requirement.

In order for SLM to be confident about the achievement of its SLA targets, it must have specific agreements with the internal and external providers. These agreements fall into two distinct types:

- Underpinning contracts (UCs);
- Operational level agreements (OLAs).

Both should be negotiated, agreed and in place before a commitment is made to the relevant SLA.

**EXAMPLE**

A local authority used the multi-level structure shown in Figure 13.1 for its Finance Department.

**Figure 13.1  Multi-level SLAs**

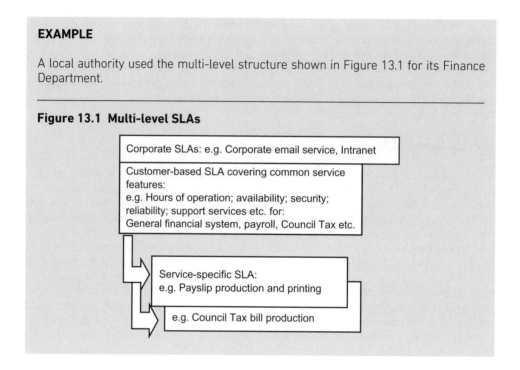

## Underpinning contracts

Where an external supplier provides services that underpin the delivery of an IT service, it is essential that the provisions of the contract with the external supplier are consistent with the targets built into any SLA that depends on the external supplier. SLM must avoid making commitments in SLAs that cannot be guaranteed because the underpinning contract with an external supplier offers a lower standard. For example, it would make little sense for SLM to base an SLA availability target on a projected server availability of 99.9 per cent when the support and maintenance contract for the server guarantees no better than 98 per cent. It is the shared responsibility of SLM and supplier management to ensure consistency. However, supplier management is accountable for renegotiating UCs where contractual commitments fall short of customer needs.

The ongoing relationship between the IT service provider and its suppliers is covered in Chapter 14 on supplier management, but it is important to recognise here that UCs must always be kept in line with the needs of the business. This means that as business requirements change, the IT service provider must ensure that UCs are renegotiated or replaced, if cost-effective to do so, to ensure they continue to serve the business.

## Operational level agreements

Many organisations find it helpful to have written agreements between different parts of the IT service provider that specify the performance targets that each part is able and prepared to underwrite. These agreements, which are known as operational level agreements (OLAs), enable SLM to have confidence in the SLAs they negotiate with customers. They are not formal contracts, and need not be written in the style of formal contractual documents, but they will make clear what should be expected of a particular section of the IT service provider.

**OPERATIONAL LEVEL AGREEMENT**

An operational level agreement (OLA) is an agreement between two teams or functions within an IT service provider. It supports the IT service provider's delivery of IT services to the customers and the service levels contained in the corresponding SLA. The OLA defines the items or services to be provided and the responsibilities of each party.

**EXAMPLE**

To facilitate effective management of incidents and communication between the service desk and second-line resolver groups, an organisation may choose to establish an OLA between these teams. The OLA would describe the responsibilities of each team and their respective commitments to each other, such as incident documentation and user communication.

## Managing service levels

Putting SLAs in place with consistent UCs and OLAs achieves nothing unless performance against the service levels is measured, monitored and reported and appropriate actions are taken to maintain and continually improve service delivery. The ongoing responsibilities of SLM are concerned with maintaining a constructive and positive relationship with IT's customers, measuring and monitoring performance against service levels, reporting and reviewing performance with the customer, dealing with changing requirements and seeking continually to improve service levels where this is cost-effective. This is not a one-sided relationship, however. SLM also has a responsibility to help its customers and the business make the most effective use of IT and to meet their obligations included in SLAs.

Reports to customers and users should be in a format that is easy to follow. SLA Monitoring charts (SLAM) are often used (sometimes referred to as a 'RAG' report based on the use of the colours red, amber and green to indicate SLA breach, warning or met, respectively). An example is shown in Figure 13.2.

SLM has responsibility for regularly reporting to the customer on performance, but will rely on other service management processes for the information: the service desk will report on the number of incidents handled and their performance in dealing with them; availability management will report on availability; capacity management will report on any capacity issues; and so on.

## Figure 13.2 An example SLAM chart

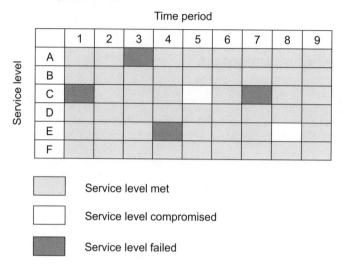

SLA review meetings

## SLA review meetings

Regular meetings with customers are a central part of SLM. They are not just an opportunity to report on and review performance, although this is one of the key issues. It is fundamentally about building and maintaining the relationship. Review meetings are a forum for exchanging information about issues of concern, such as the need for user training or worrying trends in performance or workload. They provide an opportunity for both the IT service provider and the customer to share their plans for future change: the business may be planning an expansion in usage; there may be relevant proposals in the schedule of change; IT may be planning to replace key service components or to introduce new service management elements. These meetings are a means to ensure that both sides have a common understanding and that there are no difficult surprises to manage.

Continual service improvement is a fundamental goal of service management. A key objective of the regular review meetings is to identify and agree service improvements and incorporate them into the service improvement plan and service quality plan as part of the continual improvement stage of the service lifecycle.

### SERVICE IMPROVEMENT PLAN (or PROGRAMME) (SIP)

A formal plan to introduce improvements to a process or IT service.

Service improvement plans (SIPs) are intended to find and implement ways to restore or improve service quality. They should cover all relevant services, processes and activities, and address related priorities, costs, impacts and risks. A SIP will often involve a range of initiatives (e.g. covering internal IT processes, customer training and behaviour, third-party services and so on).

# RELATIONSHIPS WITH OTHER SERVICE MANAGEMENT PROCESSES

Service level management interacts with and to an extent depends on all other service management processes. Some of these relationships are more important than others, but SLM cannot deliver to its fullest potential unless all SM processes are fully implemented and effective.

## Service desk and incident management

There are key relationships with the service desk and incident management, which, in seeking to restore service as quickly as possible following an incident, directly underpin the delivery of the service levels to which SLM has committed on behalf of the IT provider.

## Problem management

Problem management has a clear role in dealing, both reactively and proactively, with problems that might give rise to incidents that undermine the delivery of the service.

## Change management

Effective change management is clearly critical to maintaining service levels because badly managed and poorly planned change can lead to disruption of services and failure to achieve against SLAs.

## Release management

Sound release management minimises service disruption, ensures releases are deployed at times that suit the customer and minimises incidents due to releases that are either poorly planned or managed.

## Design coordination

SLM supports design coordination by developing and agreeing service level requirements and service levels that need to be incorporated into the design of the new or changed service.

## Other processes

All processes will report to SLM on issues, opportunities and performance, thereby supporting SLM in its reviews with customers.

Availability management, capacity management and service continuity management are concerned with ensuring that services continue to deliver the service levels included in the relevant SLAs. SLM, as the primary contact with the customer, will provide information on required service levels and on upcoming changes to the business. In return, these processes will report to SLM on performance and make proposals for service improvement.

## METRICS

Metrics can be used to assess both the effectiveness of the SLM process in delivering services to the standards agreed and the extent to which SLM is successful in managing the interface with the business.

Under the first heading, useful quantitative performance indicators would include:

- the frequency and severity of service breaches;
- the frequency and severity of threatened service breaches (near misses);
- the frequency and severity of breaches and threatened breaches resulting from UCs;
- the frequency and severity of breaches and threatened breaches resulting from OLAs;
- the number and percentage of service levels met;
- customer satisfaction with the process in relation to managing levels of service.

Measures under the second heading would include:

- the number and percentage of services with up-to-date SLAs;
- the frequency of service review meetings;
- the frequency of agreed reports delivered on time.

It is also important to assess customers' views on how useful the process is to them. This can be addressed through surveys, but often a more telling indication can be obtained from the level of customer representation at review meetings, the extent to which representatives change from one meeting to the next and the quality of contribution to meetings. All of these are useful pointers to how people really feel about the process.

Metrics can also be put in place to assess the efficiency and effectiveness of the SLM process. For example:

- The costs and time required to generate and agree new SLAs.
- The costs of monitoring and reporting on SLA achievements.
- The cost of monitoring and reporting of SLAs.
- The time required for developing and agreeing SLAs.
- The percentage of services covered by SLAs.
- The percentage of SLAs reviewed by their review dates.
- The number of SLAs found to be unsatisfactory and needing to be corrected.

## ROLES

The key role in SLM is the service level manager, who has responsibility for directing and managing the SLM process. The service level manager will have responsibility for the SLA framework and structure and for the overall relationship between the IT service provider and its customers and with the business. The SLM will have overall responsibility and accountability for the success of the SLM process.

In a smaller organisation, the service level manager is likely to be involved personally in developing, negotiating, agreeing and reporting on individual SLAs, in negotiating OLAs and liaising with supplier management in relation to UCs in order to ensure that these are aligned with the agreed service levels. In a larger organisation, some of these roles will be delegated to service level management staff.

The service owner is a critical SLM role with responsibility for ensuring that a specified service or group of services are delivered to the agreed service levels and has responsibility for continual service improvement and managing change for his or her services. The service owner represents the service within the organisation, ensuring the information in the service catalogue is correct and acts as an escalation point for major incidents and a focus for service improvement. The service owner has a role in defining service targets, will participate in service review meetings with the business and with IT and takes part in SLA and OLA negotiations.

Although not part of SLM, it is important to mention business relationship management (BRM) in this context. In common with SLM, BRM is responsible for maintaining an effective relationship with the business and business managers. BRM is tasked to ensure the IT service provider is meeting the overall needs of the business and consequently has a role in service portfolio management. For SLM, meeting service levels is a measure of how well the IT service provider meets the needs of the business.

Given that there is so much common ground between SLM and BRM, these roles are often combined to bring the main streams of relationship management together.

The reporting analyst is a CSI key role that is not strictly part of SLM. Nevertheless, the reporting analyst, who reviews and analyses data to assess end-to-end service achievement, identifying positive or negative trends, will often work closely with SLM.

# 14   SUPPLIER MANAGEMENT

## INTRODUCTION AND SCOPE

Few IT services today are delivered in totality by the IT service provider. For example, services relying on networks for delivery are likely to depend on a telecommunications provider for links between geographically dispersed sites; hardware maintenance will usually be in the hands of a third-party supplier; commercial software packages will be supported and maintained by external suppliers, often, but not always, the software vendor.

As discussed under service level management, the relationship between these external providers and the IT service provider is in part defined by underpinning contracts between the IT service provider and the third-party suppliers responsible for supporting services. However, supplier management, which seeks to ensure that suppliers and their services are managed in such a way that the continuing quality and good value for money of IT services is ensured, is about much more than the one-off negotiation of a support contract.

> ### SUPPLIER
>
> A third party responsible for supplying goods or services.

Supplier management is all about getting the best from suppliers in order to ensure the delivery of services meet agreed service level targets at optimal cost. It is about getting good value for money from suppliers. It recognises that there is more to a supplier relationship than the contract, seeing the relationship as a continuing and dynamic asset that not only serves the needs of today, but also helps the IT service provider respond to new challenges and risks as the commercial, technological and social environment changes around it. It recognises the need for continual service improvement and the value of productive relationships as a platform for achieving higher service quality or better value for money or both of these things.

The scope of supplier management covers the management of all suppliers to the IT service provider. In practice, this does not mean that all suppliers should be given equal attention. Some will have a lesser role in the delivery of IT services, those that provide minor services or commodity items that can be easily sourced elsewhere. Some will have a much greater impact on the IT service provider – these suppliers require more proactive management and attention, especially where their failure to deliver can have a profound effect on the ability of the IT service provider to deliver services.

## PURPOSE AND OBJECTIVES

The purpose of supplier management is to manage suppliers and the services they deliver in order to ensure the organisation gets the best value from each supplier throughout the lifecycle of the relationship with the supplier. Given the complexity of modern IT services, it is common for individual services to be provided through a mix of internal and external suppliers. Supplier management has to manage the complexity of relationships with external suppliers in such a way that they all pull in the same direction and, in doing so, deliver services that underpin the service level targets enshrined in SLAs at a cost that represents best value for the organisation. A key outcome for supplier management is to ensure that the optimum value is achieved from the relationship with a supplier – this rarely means squeezing suppliers until they have no more to offer. The purpose of supplier management is also about the longer term. The old confrontational supplier management approaches are hopefully outdated. Supplier management today has to be about building long-term relationships, ideally built around shared risk and reward models, where success in the relationship is a mutual goal – the basis of a partnership arrangement rather than simply the provision of a managed service.

This does not mean that the relationship between the organisation and its suppliers is casual. A key purpose of supplier management is to ensure that effective contracts are in place, ensuring that the supplier delivers according to the terms, conditions and delivery targets contained within the contract. What is understood by an effective contract is crucial. An effective contract is not about driving the price down to a point where the supplier cannot sustain delivery or needs to claw back revenue by holding the organisation to ransom over essential contract variations.

### EXAMPLE

One public sector organisation squeezed a key supplier on price to a point where everyone should have realised that service delivery would be at risk. Unfortunately, the organisation continued to congratulate itself on its hard negotiating tactics until the inevitable happened. The whole thing ended up in court with both sides blaming the other. Irrespective of the outcome of the court case, the IT service collapsed and the organisation was left to manage the mess.

The main objectives of supplier management are:

- to develop and maintain a supplier policy;
- to establish and manage constructive relationships with suppliers;

- to negotiate and agree contracts with suppliers that align with the needs of the business and manage these contracts through their lifecycle;
- to ensure, in collaboration with SLM, that contracts that underpin the delivery of other services are aligned with the targets contained in SLRs and SLAs;
- to manage suppler performance to ensure they deliver good value for money;
- to develop and maintain a supporting supplier and contract management information system.

## GENERAL PRINCIPLES

Supplier management is, of course, about negotiating contracts that are consistent with the needs of the business and that support the achievement of targets in the relevant SLAs. It is also about managing the longer-term relationship with suppliers and their continuing performance. It requires positive management throughout the contract lifecycle, monitoring delivery and performance to identify and deal with issues and potential problems before they occur. It involves the renegotiation, renewal and even the termination of contracts as the needs of the business change. It involves monitoring the extent to which contracts continue to deliver good value for money as the marketplace and technological options change over time and this in turn means maintaining a comprehensive base of information about the marketplace and the suppliers that populate it.

In order to benefit fully from the relationship with a supplier, the IT service provider must have a clear understanding of where it wants to be. It needs to understand and articulate its own long-term goals in the context of the business it serves, and to define the services it must design and develop in order to achieve these goals. An analysis of its own resources and capabilities against the resources and capabilities needed to deliver these services will identify areas where external assistance may be required. This analysis, along with an analysis of risks, will provide a foundation for the development of new or changing relationships with suppliers.

## CATEGORISING SUPPLIERS

More time should be spent managing key suppliers and less time on less important suppliers. This implies that suppliers should be categorised and one way to do this is by their impact on, risk to and value of the services they support or deliver as shown in Figure 14.1. One way to categorise suppliers is as follows:

- strategic
- tactical
- operational
- commodity.

**Figure 14.1 Supplier categorisation**

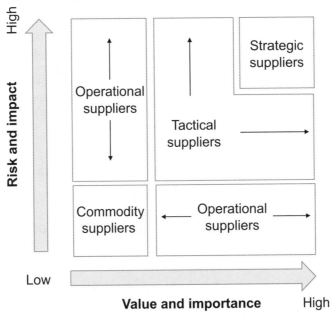

## KEY ACTIVITIES

The supplier management process should include the following key activities:

- The development, implementation and management of a supplier policy.
- The categorisation of suppliers and contracts and associated risk assessment.
- Supplier evaluation and selection.
- Contract negotiation and agreement.
- Development and maintenance of standard terms and conditions.
- Dispute management and resolution.
- Development and maintenance of a supplier and contracts management information system (SCMIS).

## THE SUPPLIER AND CONTRACT MANAGEMENT INFORMATION SYSTEM (SCMIS)

The supplier management process is governed by the IT service provider's supplier policy and strategy. These determine how the organisation will use external suppliers and the rules of engagement when it does so. It should define how suppliers should be selected and how relationships should be managed. In the public sector, for example, the rules for procurement from the private sector are enshrined in legislation in most countries and these rules should be incorporated into the supplier policy.

In common with other SM processes, sound supplier management depends on the effective management of information. In supplier management, the key information base is the supplier and contracts management information system (SCMIS), which will hold information on all suppliers and contracts, together with the goods and services provided by each supplier. The SCMIS is best implemented as a part of the configuration management system (CMS), itself part of the IT provider's service knowledge management system (SKMS). The integration of the SCMIS with the CMS enables suppliers and contracts to be linked to services, CIs and other service elements that depend on the supplier contract, enabling better risk and impact assessment and management reporting. The information in the SCMIS will also be included for reference in the service portfolio and service catalogue.

The SCMIS is used to manage suppliers and contracts throughout the contract lifecycle, providing information to, and being updated from, the key supplier management activities. It holds details of suppliers, including key contacts along with contract details including renewal and termination dates.

## RELATIONSHIPS WITH OTHER SERVICE MANAGEMENT PROCESSES

### Service level management

SLM in relation to the alignment of UCs with SLA and SLR targets, includes the renegotiation of UCs, where possible, to improve performance or reduce service costs and the investigation of breaches and near breaches of SLR and SLA targets because of unsatisfactory performance. Supplier management will also advise or liaise with SLM in relation to planned contract terminations and key supplier events such as failure, mergers and takeovers. Supplier management is also a source of information on third-party service costs, which will feed through into IT charges if relevant.

### Other service management processes

Relationships between supplier management and other SM processes include those with:

- Information security management (ISM) to ensure suppliers understand and comply with IT security policy and specific security requirements in their dealings with the organisation;
- Service portfolio management and service catalogue management to ensure that all details of suppliers, contracts and third-party services are accurately recorded and kept up to date. If these details are held with the CMDB, there will be a similar interface with CMS;
- IT service continuity management (ITSCM) in relation to contracts held for business continuity services. ITSCM may also contribute to the risk assessment of suppliers by sharing the outcome of business impact analysis (BIA);
- Financial management to ensure there are adequate finances to cover contractual commitments and for supplier management to feed information into financial management for budget development;

- CSI functions in relation to supplier service improvement plans, which may underpin the achievement of service improvement targets;
- Service strategy processes in relation to supplier policy and strategy development and the more general formulation of IT strategy;
- Service design in relation to the options for using third-party suppliers to deliver proposed services or to underpin their delivery.

In practice, it is also important for supplier management to work closely with business management, finance, procurement and legal services to ensure contracts are managed effectively throughout their lifecycle.

## ROLES

Managing the relationship with a supplier should be the responsibility of a specific person from the IT service provider, the supplier manager, although this person may manage the relationship with a number of suppliers. The time and effort allocated to the management of a given supplier and the level at which this is managed within the IT service supplier's organisation should reflect the importance of the supplier to the IT service provider's business. A supplier of minor services will generally need less attention than does a supplier with strategic importance across a range of services. For suppliers in the latter category it is good practice to adopt an open management approach based on mutual trust, where each side shares its plans with the other. This enables both sides to prepare for new challenges based on an understanding of the needs, pressures and priorities of the other partner.

This approach generally has more potential for generating value in the relationship than the traditional confrontational approach, as the supplier becomes more involved in helping the IT service provider to deliver benefit to the business. The objectives are shared risk and reward rather than blame and animosity.

The supplier manager's responsibilities include:

- maintaining a comprehensive SCMIS;
- ensuring contracts align with the business and offer good value for money;
- ensuring all suppliers and contracts offer an acceptable level of risk to the enterprise;
- managing supplier performance to ensure contractual obligations are met;
- managing contracts throughout their lifecycle, including all changes and variations.

# 15  CAPACITY MANAGEMENT

## INTRODUCTION AND SCOPE

The capacity management process is responsible for all activities related to the provision of adequate and cost-effective capacity. The scope also includes performance management.

Capacity and performance are tightly linked because although service levels are usually expressed in terms of performance (e.g. response time, throughput rate etc.), when resources run short of capacity, performance suffers.

### EXAMPLE

A good analogy is a supermarket's ability to serve its customers in a reasonable time. In order to allow shoppers to checkout without having to queue for a long time, there is a continual need to balance the number of checkout staff with the number of shoppers.

The capacity management process is mainly a proactive one because it is driven by future business need. Therefore the earlier that capacity and performance are considered in the service lifecycle, the greater the degree of confidence that a service will be able to meet the required service levels when it is transitioned into operation.

The main challenge for capacity management is to predict the demand on resources to be able to provide enough capacity to meet service levels on an ongoing basis.

### EXAMPLE

In the supermarket analogy, this means estimating the number of shoppers over the day and perhaps how many items they will buy and then scheduling staff working hours and breaks to minimise queuing.

In IT terms, this means gathering information about business plans, assessing the impact on services and underpinning resources and then buying or upgrading resources (or selling or downgrading resources if demand is falling) in time to avoid either insufficient capacity and missed service levels or excess capacity and unnecessary cost. For this reason, the capacity management process is sometimes more memorably summarised as 'having the right IT capacity in the right place at the right time and at the right cost.'

Without forward planning, achieving this balance is not possible because reacting to capacity shortfalls takes time. It takes time to gain approval to purchase, to physically acquire the capacity and then install and configure it. In the meantime, performance suffers and the business is impacted. Equally, without forward planning, capacity shortfalls may need to be tackled urgently. In such situations, there is a potential for panic buying. It is unlikely that urgent purchases are made in the most cost-effective manner.

## PURPOSE AND OBJECTIVES

In simple terms, the purpose of the capacity management process is to ensure that there are sufficient IT resources to satisfy the current and future needs of the business. This is a two-part balancing act:

- **Supply versus demand:** Sufficient resources must be available to meet the business demand and maintain service levels. This can be helped by influencing demand (through the demand management process) to make the most effective use of resources and by tuning and optimising current resources.

- **Costs versus resources:** Spend on resources must be justified by business need and resources must be used efficiently. This can be helped by considering the cost benefits of newer technology.

The purpose of the process is to provide a focal point and management responsibility for all capacity and performance-related activities in respect of both resources and services.

The primary objectives of the process are as follows:

- Produce and maintain a capacity plan, assessing the impact of changes on the plan and on the performance of services and resources.

- Contribute to meeting service levels by managing the capacity and performance of services and resources.

- Provide advice and guidance on all capacity and performance-related activities, assist with the diagnosis and resolution of related incidents and problems and propose proactive performance improvements where these are cost-justifiable.

## THE CAPACITY PLAN

The capacity plan is a key output of the process because it predicts and costs the impact of new and changing business plans on the current IT environment. This provides IT management with a reliable forecast to support decisions necessary to maintain service stability and achieve the balances described in the Introduction to this chapter. The plan is usually produced annually and synchronised to IT financial planning. Updates may be routinely produced once or twice a year or in response to unexpected changes and new requirements.

The accuracy of the plan relies on the level of understanding of the utilisation and capacity of the components supporting the services and the ability to predict their impact on service performance when the demand on them changes. This in turn is dependent on accurate configuration information and the ability to model the interaction between components and workload.

Some organisations base their plan on a simple extrapolation of current usage with little or no reference to business activities or plans. However, this has been likened to steering a car by looking out of the back window. What has happened in the past is not necessarily a useful guide to what might happen in the future.

## THE THREE SUB-PROCESSES OF CAPACITY MANAGEMENT

Capacity management has three sub-processes to reflect the different activities needed to prepare the capacity plan. Each of these requires different skills which in larger organisations might be undertaken by different people. Figure 15.1 shows how the sub-processes fit together and their contribution to the capacity management process.

### Business capacity management

The business capacity management sub-process analyses the patterns of business activity (PBAs) coming from demand management. These PBAs show both the volume of work and how this volume fluctuates over time. Business capacity management then gathers information about new business activities such as launching a new product, relocating a department or opening a new facility. This may be provided directly from business managers to the capacity management team or may come from the service option produced for the service portfolio. Superimposing forecasts of new activities on top of patterns of current usage helps this sub-process to provide service capacity management with an accurate projection of changing business activities over time.

### Service capacity management

Service capacity management seeks to correlate business activity and service usage. For example, a call centre's usage of the customer relationship management (CRM) service is probably dependent on the number of customers, how often they call and what information they require. The relationship between these factors and CRM service usage can be mapped or modelled so that the impact of business activity changes can be predicted in terms of service performance (e.g. transaction response times) over time.

### Component capacity management

When service capacity management identifies that service levels will fall below target, component capacity management is the sub-process responsible for identifying the

**Figure 15.1 Capacity management overview with sub-processes**

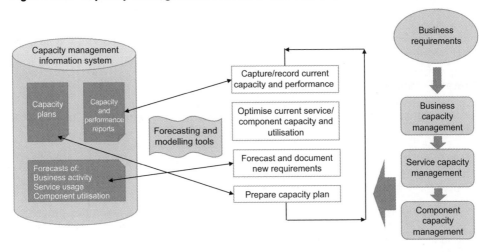

necessary changes to the technical infrastructure to maintain service levels. To be fully effective, configuration information is necessary to understand which components (configuration items) support which services. The utilisation of these components should be continually monitored against their capacity and, ideally, an alert generated when a threshold is reached that could cause service levels to be missed.

## RELATIONSHIPS WITH OTHER SERVICE MANAGEMENT PROCESSES

Capacity management has a close relationship with many of the other processes. These are detailed below.

### Financial management

Capacity management contributes to financial management predominantly via the capacity plan. The capacity plan describes and financially quantifies the resources required to deliver the committed level of service. Where there is a need to acquire new resources, capacity management predicts how much additional resource will be required and at what point in time. This allows financial management to budget for the cost of the new resources. During the budget year, as new resources are needed, capacity management will be instrumental in providing the justification for the actual purchase in terms of size, time and cost.

### Service level management

The feedback that the capacity manager receives from business representatives in respect of their business plans and forecasts needs to be considered with the service level requirements gathered by the service level manager. Capacity management must therefore take into consideration the service level requirements when forecasting the resources needed to support new and growing services. The relationship works both ways, however. When the service level manager is discussing service level requirements with the business, the capacity and performance requirements are costed by capacity management so that the business can make an informed decision regarding the balance between performance and cost. This is the control mechanism that prevents the business from asking for or demanding ever increasing levels of performance from the IT systems.

## Demand management

Demand management works closely with and supports capacity management in several ways:

- By helping to understand patterns of business activity and user profiles, demand management helps capacity management more accurately predict and plan for the consumption of resources for new users.
- By finding ways to smooth out peak loads, demand management helps capacity management make the most cost-effective use of existing resources and helps to defer the purchase of new resources.
- During times of peak load, demand management can dynamically throttle usage to maintain service levels, for example by restricting the number of concurrent users of an online system to protect response times.

## IT service continuity management

Capacity management contributes to the service continuity management process by sharing plans and modelling output to help ensure that the alternative facilities provided by service continuity management remain in line with the live environment and can continue to provide contingency in the event of being invoked.

## Change and release management

The introduction of new resources to maintain appropriate levels of capacity and performance is managed through both change management and release and deployment management. These processes manage the impact of the change on other CIs. Likewise, capacity management supports change management by looking at the capacity and performance implications of the planned change and ensuring adequate capacity exists to accommodate subsequent deployment of the corresponding release.

## Service asset and configuration management

Service asset and configuration management provides the information about CI status, specification and relationships that is clearly vital to capacity management activities such as modelling, planning and forecasting.

## Availability management

Capacity management supports availability management because a shortage of capacity in a resource or service can impact availability.

### Incident and problem management

Capacity management obviously supports incident and problem management where issues are capacity related.

## METRICS

The following metrics can be used to confirm the effectiveness of the process in providing the appropriate level of resources:

- The number of SLA breaches (or loss of user time) caused through inadequate capacity (e.g. performance below target due to lack of capacity).
- The number of incidents resulting from a lack of capacity or poor performance.

The following metrics can be used in respect of properly fulfilling the planning role:

- The number of unplanned purchases required to provide adequate capacity or performance.
- The percentage accuracy of actual versus planned spend as given in the capacity plan.
- The percentage of excess capacity (by resource type or CI).
- The number of new or changed services implemented without capacity or performance-related issues.
- The actual business demand as a percentage of forecast demand.

The following metric can be used in respect of monitoring performance:

- The percentage of CIs monitored for performance.

## ROLES

The capacity manager is responsible for the process. However, the scope is broad and may therefore be split between two or more capacity analysts: one is responsible for maintaining a dialogue with business representatives and the service level manager to identify new and changing business requirements; another is likely to fulfil the more technical role of analysing the current and predicted load on performance levels (e.g. through modelling techniques).

# 16   AVAILABILITY MANAGEMENT

## INTRODUCTION AND SCOPE

The availability of IT services is the most basic requirement in any organisation. Since organisations are often so dependent on their IT services for so many business functions, if the IT service isn't available, the business of the organisation effectively stops. Availability management is primarily a proactive process with a primary purpose of cost-effectively meeting the availability requirements the business has of its IT services both now and in the future.

If an organisation has any doubts about the need for investing in availability management, consider the impact of being without vital business functions that rely on the availability of IT services. Financially, the cost of service downtime can be measured in terms of lost user time as follows:

number of incidents × average outage duration × average number of users affected × average employment cost per user

### EXAMPLE

Forty incidents a week with an average outage of 40 minutes each, affecting on average 40 users at an employment cost of €40k each, incurs lost user time equivalent to more than €1.2 million per annum.

However, even the cost of lost user time can be small compared with the lost opportunity cost or consequential loss of not being able to trade during this downtime. There are obviously other industry sectors such as health care and security where the impact of losing key IT services is far more significant than a financial loss.

Availability management can be extremely effective in identifying and eliminating potential causes of lost availability and in a commercial organisation it will undoubtedly save more money than it costs.

## PURPOSE AND OBJECTIVES

The purpose of availability management is to ensure that service availability matches business needs cost-effectively.

The primary objectives for the process are:

- to prepare and maintain the availability plan;
- to monitor availability levels and the status of resources and services to identify potential and actual availability issues and prevent or minimise any consequent business interruptions;
- to manage the availability of services and resources to meet agreed service levels;
- to provide a focal point and management responsibility for all availability-related activities in respect of both resources and services;
- to assist with the investigation and resolution of availability-related incidents and problems;
- to assess the impact of changes on availability levels and plans;
- to proactively improve availability where the cost is justified.

## VITAL BUSINESS FUNCTIONS

### VITAL BUSINESS FUNCTION

A vital business function is that element of a business process critical to the success of the business.

The basic principle is that the more critical a business function is, the more important it is for IT to design in resilience and availability to supporting IT services. However, if IT designs in availability at an unnecessarily high level, this incurs excess service costs. The availability requirement is defined by the business and should be documented within the service level agreement.

## HOW COMPONENT AVAILABILITY AFFECTS SERVICE AVAILABILITY

In order to understand the potential for the failure of an IT service, it is first necessary to identify the components or configuration items on which the service depends. Clearly, for the service to be available, all the components that contribute to the hosting and delivery of the service must be available. In a simple model where each component is connected in series (i.e. one behind the other), the availability of the service is the product of the availability of the components on which it runs.

### EXAMPLE

If three components are required to deliver a service and each has an availability of 98.0 per cent, the availability of the service is

$$98.0\% \times 98.0\% \times 98.0\% = 94.1\%.$$

This equates to a figure of 1 hour, 25 minutes a day.

Availability management, as a proactive process, learns of business requirements from the service level manager and then seeks to ensure that services and the components on which they depend are capable of meeting this requirement. Designing-in availability to new services is always more cost-effective than making changes after the service is deployed, so availability management needs to be actively involved at the design stage. The two most effective ways to design-in the required level of availability are to select components with an adequate specification and to design the systems to reduce the dependency on individual components.

**EXAMPLE**

When two identical components are put in parallel, as shown in Figure 16.1, the service only fails if both components fail.

---

**Figure 16.1  Components in parallel**

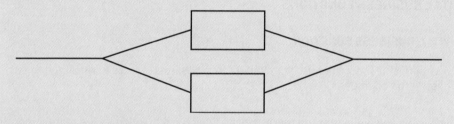

Therefore if each component in this example has an availability of 98.0 per cent, then the availability of the service is

$$1 - [(1 - 0.98) \times (1 - 0.98)] = 99.96\%.$$

Applying this design to our earlier example, three components each with a parallel back up having the same availability generates an overall service availability of

$$99.96\% \times 99.96\% \times 99.96\% = 99.88\%$$

instead of 94.1% or less than 2 minutes per day and a fifty-fold improvement.

In this way, single points of failure can be eliminated and the end-to-end availability improved.

Other methods for improving the availability of services include the use of fault tolerant components and systems that mask the effect of a component failure or allow one or more components to be taken out of service (e.g. for maintenance or replacement).

## PROACTIVE AVAILABILITY MANAGEMENT TECHNIQUES

There are a number of techniques used by availability management that look to prevent service outages by identifying and eliminating the sources of service failures. One of these is the availability plan, wherein availability management identifies and costs the requirements for new and upgraded resources necessary to deliver the required levels of availability. The availability plan will also include an assessment of the risks of service interruption and failure and appropriate actions necessary to mitigate those risks.

Risk analysis and management are important across IT service management, especially in processes and activities that concern service availability. These include availability management, security management and IT service continuity management, which is covered in the next chapter where a fuller discussion of risk analysis and management is included.

Another technique is to assess the impact of requests for change (RFCs) to understand their potential to interrupt services and find ways to prevent this occurring.

Other proactive techniques include advising on cost-effective new technology to improve availability and providing advice and guidance to other areas of IT and the business on all availability-related aspects.

## REACTIVE AVAILABILITY MANAGEMENT

On a reactive basis, availability management helps incident and problem management to diagnose and resolve availability-related incidents and problems. Of course, the understanding gained from the resolution of such problems can often contribute to proactive initiatives to prevent similar occurrences in the future.

Availability management also monitors, measures, reports and reviews service and component availability to ensure that service levels continue to be met and respond to any outages or potential service level breaches. In this respect, there is a link to the event management process.

## RELATIONSHIPS WITH OTHER SERVICE MANAGEMENT PROCESSES

### Service asset and configuration management

Availability management is heavily reliant on service asset and configuration management to identify the components used in delivering a service, their relationship with one another and their technical specifications.

### IT service continuity management

Availability management is closely related to IT service continuity management because invoking a continuity plan is simply another form of maintaining the availability of services in extreme situations. Both processes need to identify vital business functions and use risk management techniques to define appropriate responses.

## Capacity management

Availability management is supported by capacity management because a shortage of capacity in a resource or service can impact availability.

## Access management and information security management

Access management and information security management are both concerned with preventing unauthorised access and permitting authorised access. Availability of a service depends on the ability of the user to access the service and negotiate the security controls according to their authority.

## Change management and release and deployment management

Change management as well as release and deployment management must ensure that availability management is aware of planned changes and their potential to impact on the availability of services.

## Service level management

Availability management supports service level management by managing the IT resources to meet cost-effectively agreed service levels and by contributing to the design of new and changed services to ensure the appropriate levels of availability are built-in.

## Event, incident and problem management

Reactively, availability management takes feeds from event management to warn of actual and impending failures and supports incident and problem management in the diagnosis and resolution of availability-related incidents and problems.

## METRICS

There are a number of measures used to assess and report the performance of a service or component in respect of it being available.

Availability is defined as the ability of a service or component to perform its required function when needed. It is usually calculated as a percentage:

$$\text{percentage availability} = \frac{\text{agreed service time} - \text{downtime}}{\text{agreed service time}} \times 100\%$$

(N.B. Downtime outside agreed service time is not included.)

**Reliability** is a measure of how long a service or component can perform its required function without interruption. In simple terms – the average up-time. It is usually calculated in one of two ways:

$$\text{mean time between system incidents (MTBSI)} = \frac{\text{available time}}{\text{number of breaks}}$$

$$\text{mean time between failures (MTBF)} = \frac{\text{available time} - \text{total downtime}}{\text{number of breaks}}$$

**Maintainability** is a measure of how quickly a service or component can be restored to its working state after a failure. In simple terms – the average down-time. It is usually calculated as:

$$\text{mean time to restore service (MTRS)} = \frac{\text{total downtime}}{\text{number of breaks}}$$

(N.B. Availability, reliability and maintainability measures all need to include a time interval, typically hours.)

**Serviceability** is a measure of a third-party provider's ability to meet their contracted support commitments in terms of availability, reliability and maintainability.

Each of these measures is subject to scrutiny and appropriate actions by availability management in order to minimise interruptions to services and service outages both proactively and reactively. The extent to which a service is vital to the business will determine the level of availability and resilience applied. Those business functions considered very important are known as vital business functions (VBFs) and it is these on which availability management will be most focused.

In relation to the expanded incident lifecycle, the following metrics are useful:

- Incident detection time;
- Incident diagnosis time;
- Incident repair time;
- Incident recovery time;
- Incident restoration time;
- Incident resolution time.

## ROLES

The availability manager is responsible for ensuring that the purpose and objectives of the process are met. Responsibilities include:

- ensuring service levels in respect of availability are met for all current and new services;
- responding to availability-related incidents and problems;

- ensuring that appropriate CIs and services are monitored for availability through event management;
- specifying appropriate levels of component reliability, maintainability and serviceability;
- reporting availability performance against service levels;
- creating and maintaining the availability plan;
- the continual improvement of the availability management process;
- cost-justifying availability requirements with financial management;
- attending change advisory board (CAB) meetings as required and assessing requests for change for their impact on availability.

## KEY PERFORMANCE INDICATORS

In addition to the specific measures above, availability management can use a range of key performance indicators (KPIs) to demonstrate continual improvement:

- Percentage reduction in service unavailability;
- Percentage increase in service reliability;
- Percentage improvement in end-to-end availability;
- Percentage reduction in the number of service breaks;
- Percentage reduction in lost user time due to unavailability of services;
- Percentage reduction in third-party contract breaches of availability service levels.

# 17 IT SERVICE CONTINUITY MANAGEMENT

## INTRODUCTION AND SCOPE

Most organisations' dependency on their IT systems is such that the loss of key applications or infrastructure could cause the company to fail within days if not earlier. Because of this, organisations need to plan how they will recover their key systems within an appropriate timescale in the event of a failure. This is the focus of the IT service continuity management (ITSCM) process.

Organisations can of course suffer from the loss of systems other than IT systems and should therefore have a general business continuity plan that protects against any eventuality that could threaten its vital business functions (VBFs). ITSCM should therefore support and align with the organisation's business continuity management (BCM) process where this exists.

## PURPOSE AND OBJECTIVES

The purpose of ITSCM is to support business continuity management by ensuring that the IT resources, systems and services can be reinstated within agreed timescales in the event of a major incident. This is achieved by creating and maintaining the necessary facilities and recovery capabilities.

The objectives of the process are:

- to create and maintain the IT service continuity plans and recovery plans;
- to carry out regular business impact analysis (BIA) exercises to ensure that the plans remain aligned with changing business requirements;
- to carry out regular risk analysis and management exercises to determine the potential for failure and identify and implement appropriate responses that meet agreed business continuity targets;
- to assess the impact of changes and take appropriate action to continue to provide the required level of protection;
- to ensure that the appropriate third-party contracts and agreements are in place and kept up to date to maintain the continuity and recovery plans;
- to proactively enhance recovery capabilities where it is cost-effective to do so;
- to provide advice and guidance on continuity and recovery-related issues.

# KEY ACTIVITIES

## The service continuity management lifecycle

Establishing and maintaining ITSCM is a cyclical process that ensures continued alignment with business continuity plans and business priorities. This process is shown in Figure 17.1.

The first two steps, initiation and then requirements and strategy, mainly relate to BCM. ITSCM begins with producing an ITSCM strategy to underpin the BCM strategy. The ITSCM strategy must ensure that cost-effective plans exist to recover IT services and any required IT infrastructure necessary to maintain VBFs.

**Figure 17.1 ITSCM process**

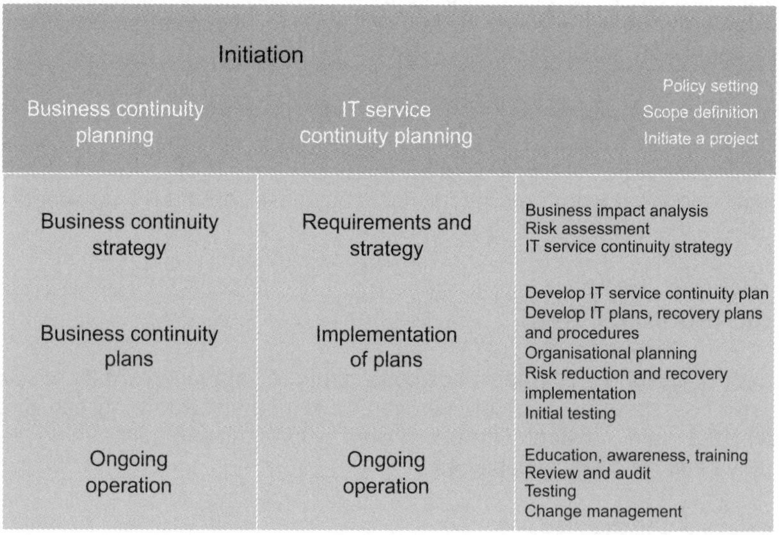

| Initiation | | |
|---|---|---|
| Business continuity planning | IT service continuity planning | Policy setting<br>Scope definition<br>Initiate a project |
| Business continuity strategy | Requirements and strategy | Business impact analysis<br>Risk assessment<br>IT service continuity strategy |
| Business continuity plans | Implementation of plans | Develop IT service continuity plan<br>Develop IT plans, recovery plans and procedures<br>Organisational planning<br>Risk reduction and recovery implementation<br>Initial testing |
| Ongoing operation | Ongoing operation | Education, awareness, training<br>Review and audit<br>Testing<br>Change management |

The situation is more complex where some or all of the IT services are outsourced to another organisation. In this case, the ITSCM manager must ensure that the outsourcer's continuity and recovery plans meet the objectives and timescales of the business.

## Business impact analysis

Business impact analysis (BIA) is the activity performed by ITSCM, often together with availability management, that works with the business to understand the impact on the organisation of suffering degraded service or losing an IT service or component. The analysis will identify business functions that are critical to the success of the organisation (VBFs) and it is these functions that ITSCM must protect from the impact of an IT failure. The business will define the recovery requirement for these functions that ITSCM must address through its IT continuity plans. Over time, the importance of business functions can change and new ones appear, so ITSCM must undertake regular BIA exercises and feed the results back into the continuity plans to ensure they remain appropriate and up to date.

## Risk analysis and management

The first step in protecting VBFs is to understand their dependency on the IT services and infrastructure. This information can be discovered from the configuration management system. Next, ITSCM must consider a number of factors:

- What could cause a service or component to fail? Examples can include fire, flood and security breaches in addition to simple mechanical or electrical failure.

- What is the likelihood of this happening? In other words, what are the chances that each of the events defined above could occur?

- What is the impact of such an occurrence? If one of the events did occur, what effect would this have on the business? This might be expressed in terms of the impact on its reputation, its customers, its finances or its legal or compliance requirements, for example.

The outcome of these considerations will determine the appropriate actions ITSCM has to take to mitigate the risks adequately and cost-effectively. Typically, the greater the likelihood of failure and the greater the impact, the greater the level of protection needed and the greater the justification for the necessary expense.

The above underlines the importance of risk analysis and management to ITSCM.

> **RISK**
>
> An event that could cause damage or loss, or affect the ability to meet objectives. A risk is measured by the probability of the event, the vulnerability of the asset to that event and the impact it would have if it occurred.

The first stage of risk analysis and management is to identify potential threats to an asset or service, estimate the probability that the threat might materialise, assess how vulnerable the asset or service is to these threats and to assess the impact should the threat materialise. For example, as identified above, flood is one example of a threat that might be relevant to an asset such as a data centre. We would determine the probability that the centre might be flooded, assess the vulnerability of the data centre to flooding and the impact on the organisation if it did flood. Putting all these together would give us a measure of risk.

The second part of risk management is doing something about the risks identified. Generally, we can do a number of things about risks:

- Some risks can just be accepted and provision made in case the worst happens. If we cannot insure our data centre because it sits in a flood plain, we may decide to hold a contingency fund in case it does flood.

- We can avoid or eliminate the risk; for example, we can eliminate the risk to our data centre by deciding to go back to manual processing. This is not always a practical solution.

- We can transfer the risk to somebody else, for example by taking out insurance or by outsourcing the data centre and disaster recovery.

- We can reduce the risk by reducing the probability of the threat or by reducing the severity if the risk materialises. For our data centre we might move it to the top of a hill to reduce the probability of a flood or reduce the impact of a flood by replacing under floor cables with fibre optics.

In many cases, the response to risk will be a combination of all or some of these options, with a balance being established between the business' tolerance to risks and the cost of countermeasures.

A key issue for IT service management, and ITSCM in particular, is to have some way of analysing and managing risk. The best and safest approach is to use a tried and tested framework that covers all aspects of risk identification and management. Management of Risk (M_o_R®), a part of the Best Practice Guidance portfolio published by Axelos is a recommended framework.

## RELATIONSHIPS WITH OTHER SERVICE MANAGEMENT PROCESSES

### Availability management

There is clearly an overlap between the ITSCM process and the availability management process. The distinction is that availability management is primarily concerned with maintaining the availability of VBFs, whereas ITSCM provides contingency in the event of a failure that either availability management could not prevent or from which IT could not quickly recover.

### Change management

Changes need to be assessed for their impact on continuity plans and consequent changes incorporated into the change planning. The continuity plan itself is subject to change control.

### Service level management

Service level management will provide advice on the definition of VBFs and the expectations of the business with regard to the permissible time delays in the restoration of services.

### Capacity management

Capacity management helps to ensure adequate resources are available to accommodate services after the continuity plan is invoked and that agreed service levels can be maintained in this situation.

## Asset and configuration management

Configuration management maintains records of recovery CIs, their status and specification.

### Information security management

The potential for a security breach to cause a major incident means that information security management contributes to the BIA and risk analysis activities.

## METRICS

Metrics that can be used to measure the performance of the ITSCM service and process in respect of the effectiveness and preparedness of the organisation are as follows:

- The number of services not covered by the continuity and recovery plans (that should be covered).
- The number of issues identified in the last continuity test that remain to be addressed.
- The number of errors found in an audit of the information in lists of key people, their responsibilities and contact details.

## ROLES

The IT service continuity manager is responsible for ensuring that the objectives of the process are met. Their activities therefore include:

- undertaking BIA and risk management exercises for both existing and new services;
- implementing and maintaining the ITSCM process and continuity strategy and maintaining the alignment with business continuity planning;
- preparing and maintaining the continuity and recovery plans and ensuring that these continue to support the organisation's business continuity strategy and plans;
- regularly testing the plans for effectiveness, reviewing the results and taking action to overcome any identified deficiencies;
- ensuring that any personnel who have a role in transitioning from one location to another are fully trained and aware of their responsibilities;
- managing third-party suppliers of recovery equipment and facilities to maintain the integrity of the continuity and recovery plans;
- attending change advisory board (CAB) meetings as required and assessing changes for their impact on the plans and updating the plans accordingly;
- managing the continuity plan during invocation and restoring the service back to the primary or other designated facility.

# 18  INFORMATION SECURITY MANAGEMENT AND ACCESS MANAGEMENT

## INTRODUCTION AND SCOPE

The security of data and information is of vital importance to any organisation and it is therefore a business decision as to what information should be protected and to what level. The business's approach to the protection and use of data should be contained in a security policy to which everyone in the organisation should have access and the contents of which everyone should be aware. The system in place to enforce the security policy and ensure that the business's IT security objectives are met is known as the information security management system (ISMS). Information security management supports corporate governance by ensuring that information security risks are properly managed.

Information security management and access management are separate processes in service management in different parts of the service lifecycle but are covered together in this chapter because of their common purpose.

## PURPOSE AND OBJECTIVES

The two processes, information security management and access management have a common objective in that both are concerned with making sure that only the right people get to see information, but information security management, which is a fundamental part of the governance framework, has a much broader remit.

The objective of the information security management process is to make sure that IT security is consistent with business security, ensuring that information security is effectively managed in all service and service management activities and that information resources have effective stewardship and are properly used. This includes the identification and management of information security risks.

The purpose of information security management is primarily to be a focal point for the management of all activities concerned with information security. This is not just about protecting information resources today. It is about putting in place, maintaining and enforcing an effective information security policy. It is about understanding how the business will develop, anticipating the risks it will face, articulating how legislation and regulation will affect security requirements and making sure that information security management is able to meet these challenges of the future.

Information security management ensures an effective information security policy is in place and enforced through effective, documented security controls that apply not only to in-house employees, but also to suppliers and others who have business/contact with the organisation. It must ensure that any security breaches are managed promptly and effectively, and that risks are identified and documented and lessons are learned accordingly.

Access management is concerned with the management of people's rights of access to information. As such it has common purpose not only with information security management, but also with availability management, giving practical effect to the policies and requirements of both processes. Its purpose is to ensure that the confidentiality, integrity and availability of information are effectively managed across the organisation. Data and information must not only be protected against unauthorised access and the possibility of it being stolen or changed. It must also be readily available to those who are authorised to access it.

A key part of access management is the management of people's rights to access information and services. People who have the right, in terms of business policy and need, to access information should have that right implemented through access controls. These rights must be consistent with relevant legislation, such as data protection legislation, and must be kept under review and changed or revoked when a person's status changes within the organisation, or when a material risk is identified.

## EXAMPLE

A doctor needs access to a patient's notes to help diagnose the possible cause of an illness and prescribe the appropriate remedy, but the confidentiality of these notes needs to be protected against access by unauthorised users. However, the patient may have a legal right to reserve access to certain information to specified individuals (e.g. HIV status, abortions, mental illness and so on).

In order for access rights to have proper effect and value, access management must ensure that people can be properly identified: that each person has a unique identity to which their rights can be attached and to which activities, legitimate or otherwise, can be traced. Identity management is critical to effective access management, preventing, for example one person from pretending to be another and hijacking their rights to access and change information or, some would say even more importantly, to create new information. Organisations must take action to manage circumstance where access controls may be bypassed, for example where software developers require access to live systems during incident management.

## EXAMPLE

In one organisation, access to payroll information was very tightly controlled, but software developers fixing faults in what was a very old piece of software had full access to all parts of the system, with the ability to access, change and create records.

The security objective of an organisation is usually considered to be met when the availability, confidentiality, integrity and authenticity and non-repudiation are under control. These are defined below:

- **Availability:** Information is accessible and usable when required and the host systems can resist attacks and recover from or prevent failures.

- **Confidentiality:** Information is accessible only to those with authorised access.

- **Integrity:** Information is protected against unauthorised modification and is therefore complete and accurate.

- **Authenticity:** Authenticity is about the correct labelling or attributing of data and information to prevent, for example, the originator of an email making it appear that the email came from someone else. Authenticity is about ensuring that business transactions and information exchanges between enterprises or with partners, can be trusted.

- **Non-repudiation:** The ability to prevent the originator of a transaction falsely denying that they originated it or to prevent the receiver falsely denying having received it.

## THE INFORMATION SECURITY POLICY

The information security policy should support and be aligned to the business security policy. It should include policies covering the use of IT assets, email, the internet, important documents, remote access, access by third parties (such as suppliers) and asset disposal. In addition, it defines the approach to resetting passwords, maintaining anti-virus controls and classifying information. These policies should be available to all customers and users, as well as to IT staff, and compliance to the policy should be referenced in all internal agreements and external contracts. The policy should be reviewed and revised on at least an annual basis.

## THE INFORMATION SECURITY MANAGEMENT SYSTEM

The information security management system (ISMS – also referred to as the security framework) helps establish a cost-effective security programme to support business objectives. Figure 18.1 shows an example framework widely used and based on the ISO 27001 standard that gives the five stages of the ISMS and the scope of each stage.

The objective of the ISMS is to ensure that appropriate controls, tools and procedures are established to support the information security policy.

## ACCESS MANAGEMENT

Access management is the process of controlling access to data and information to ensure that authorised users have timely access while preventing access by unauthorised users. The access management process may be the responsibility of a dedicated function but is usually carried out by all technical and application management functions.

**Figure 18.1 ISMS framework**

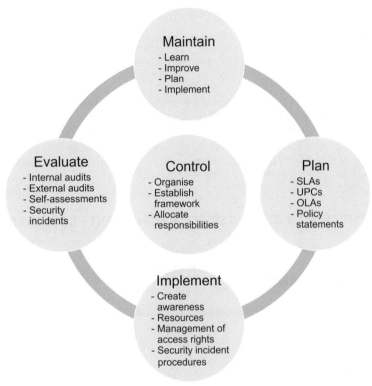

If the service desk is operating as the single point of contact, it is usual that it should receive any service requests for new or changed access rights and may also be author-ised by the owner of the security policy to grant these rights. Typically this occurs when a new person joins the organisation or a new supplier is engaged, but it may also occur when someone moves from one department to another or changes role. Access rights should be withdrawn when someone leaves the organisation.

The access management process should include monitoring access to secure informa-tion so that in the event of a security-related incident arising, the cause can be traced and any security risks discovered can be removed. Monitoring will also identify unau-thorised access attempts and instances of password errors as indications of possible security threats.

## FACILITIES MANAGEMENT – THE CONTROL OF PHYSICAL ACCESS

Information security management defines the access control policy and identifies the necessary physical security measures and who should have access to which site (e.g. the data centre). Facilities management is responsible for enforcing this policy. The major components of physical access control are:

- the installation, maintenance and management of physical access security controls such as locks and barriers and surveillance equipment;

- monitoring of physical access to protected areas;

- physical security staffing;

- maintenance of floor plans showing areas of restricted access and the relevant security controls.

One of the most common means of breaching physical security is by 'social engineering': a rather grandiose term that usually refers simply to talking your way into a secure facility (e.g. by posing as a legitimate contractor, posing as someone else or simply following a legitimate person through an open door). For this reason, security access must not only be controlled appropriately but also continually monitored so that such breaches can be detected and security controls improved.

## RELATIONSHIPS WITH OTHER SERVICE MANAGEMENT PROCESSES

To one extent or another, all other processes interface with security management.

### Availability management

Information security and access management are key contributors to availability management because without the right level of protection, the availability and integrity of data and systems is compromised.

### Service desk

The service desk usually has the authority to respond to requests for changes to access rights and passwords and therefore contributes to the operational management of security.

### Other processes

Other process interfaces are with:

- incident and problem management (response to and resolution of security-related issues);

- IT service continuity management (a design consideration and a risk during testing);

- change management (impact assessment on security controls);

- configuration management (assistance with security classification for CIs);

- capacity management (when introducing new technology);

- supplier management (to ensure maintenance of security controls for operational activities carried out by third parties).

## METRICS

Security management metrics are needed to ensure that the organisation can meet both internal and external security requirements found in SLAs, contracts, legislation and governance. Metrics that can be used for this purpose include:

- the number of security-related incidents per unit of time;
- the percentage of security-related incidents that impacted services or users;
- the number of security audit issues and risks identified;
- the percentage of security audit issues and risks resolved;
- the number of changes and releases backed-out because of security issues;
- the average time to install security patches.

## ROLES

The IT security manager is responsible for defining the information security policy and establishing the ISMS. Once these are in place, it is the IT security manager's job to ensure that all the proper controls are in place, people are aware of the policy and their responsibilities and that the security system is functioning correctly. The IT security manager is the focal point for all security issues.

Service operation teams are responsible for conducting day-to-day activities to manage operational security. It is important that these roles are kept separate from those of security management to prevent a conflict of interest. Operation roles include:

- policing and reporting;
- providing technical support and assistance;
- managing security controls;
- screening and vetting individuals;
- providing training and awareness;
- ensuring that security controls are appropriately referenced in operational documentation.

The facilities manager is usually responsible for physical security at an organisation's sites and computer facilities.

# 19 TRANSITION PLANNING AND SUPPORT

## INTRODUCTION AND SCOPE

Given the importance of transitioning services correctly into the live environment, it is not surprising that one of the key processes in this phase involves planning of all activities thoroughly and ensuring that all necessary resources are made available as and where they are required.

The key input to transition planning is the service design package, which contains all the relevant detail about the change.

Although it is not responsible for the detailed planning of activities within individual changes or releases, transition planning and support has a broad scope that includes:

- establishing policies, standards and models for service transition activities and processes;
- overseeing the progress of major changes through all the service transition processes;
- coordinating and prioritising resources to enable multiple transitions to be managed without conflict;
- budgeting for future requirements for service transition;
- reviewing and improving the performance of transition planning and support activities;
- ensuring that service transition is coordinated with programme and project management, service design and service development activities.

## PURPOSE, OBJECTIVES AND VALUE

The purpose of this process is to plan and coordinate service transitions and the resources required.

The objectives of transition planning and support are to:

- plan and coordinate the resources to ensure that the designed strategic requirements are achieved in operations;

- coordinate transition activities and processes across projects, suppliers and service teams;

- ensure new or changed services are introduced within budget, on time and with the right quality;

- ensure that new architectures, technology, processes and measurement methods are implemented correctly;

- ensure that the common framework of standard reusable processes and supporting systems is adopted by all;

- provide clear and comprehensive plans that enable customer and business change projects to align their activities with the service transition plans;

- identify, manage and control risks, minimising the chance of failure and disruption across transition activities;

- reporting service transition issues, risks and deviations to the appropriate stakeholders and decision makers;

- monitor and improve the performance of the transition activities.

Most value is derived from the individual changes or new services deployed. Effective transition planning enables the service provider to support concurrent changes and ensure the efficient coordination of activities and resources across multiple projects and teams.


## KEY ACTIVITIES

The output from the service design phase is a service design package (SDP), which includes much of the information that is required by the service transition teams. This includes:

- the service charter, describing the expected utility and warranty;

- outline budgets and timescales;

- service specifications and models;

- the chosen architectural design, including any known constraints;

- the definition and design of each specific release;

- how the service components will be assembled and integrated into a release package;

- release and deployment management plans;

- the service acceptance criteria.

### Service transition lifecycle stages

Each SDP should define the lifecycle stages for transitioning this service. Movement through it should be subject to formal checks (often as 'quality gates') against defined entry and exit criteria. Typical stages might include:

- acquire and test new configuration items (CIs) and components;
- build and component test;
- service release test;
- service operational readiness test;
- deployment;
- early-life support;
- review and close service transition.

## Preparing for service transition

Service transition preparation activities include:

- reviewing and acceptance of inputs from the other service lifecycle stages;
- reviewing and checking the input deliverables (e.g. change proposal, SDP, service acceptance criteria and evaluation report);
- identifying, raising and scheduling requests for change (RFCs);
- checking that the configuration baselines are recorded in the configuration management system (CMS) before the start of service transition;
- checking transition readiness.

## Planning an individual service transition

A service transition plan describes the tasks and activities required to release and deploy a release into the test environments and into production, including:

- work environment and infrastructure for the service transition;
- schedule of milestones, handover and delivery dates;
- activities and tasks to be performed;
- staffing, resource requirements, budgets and timescales at each stage;
- issues and risks to be managed;
- lead times and contingency.

## Integrated planning

Good planning and management are essential for successful deployment of a release into production across distributed environments and locations. It is important to maintain an integrated set of transition plans that are linked to lower level plans, such as release build and test plans. These plans should be integrated with the change schedule and release and deployment management plans. Establishing good quality plans at the outset enables service transition to manage and coordinate the service transition resources (e.g. resource allocation, utilisation, budgeting and accounting).

## Reviewing the plans

All plans should be reviewed. Wherever possible, an element of contingency should be included based on experience, including knowledge of seasonal variations and geographic factors, rather than relying on supplier assertion. This applies even more for internal suppliers where there is no formal contract.

Before starting the release, the service transition planning role should verify the plans, check that they are up to date, have been agreed and authorised by all relevant parties, and include all relevant detail (dates, deliverables etc.). It is also necessary to check that all costs and organisational, technical and commercial aspects have been considered and that overall risks have been assessed. Configuration items need checking for compatibility with each other and the target environment. People must understand and be able to implement the plans. Finally, checks should be made to ensure that no business or design changes have rendered the release inappropriate.

## Providing transition process support

Major activities include:

- providing, or arranging to be made available, relevant advice and guidance to project teams and those performing the underlying tasks;
- administration for managing service transition changes and work orders, issues, risks, deviations and waivers, support for tools and service transition processes, as well as performance;
- managing communication by executing a communication plan defining the objectives of the communication, defined stakeholders, content for each type, frequency (which may vary for each stakeholder group at different stages), format (newsletters, posters, emails, reports, presentations etc.) and how success will be measured.

## Progress monitoring and reporting

Service transition activities should be monitored against the intentions set out in the transition model and plan to ensure conformance. Management reports on the status of each transition will help to identify when there are significant variances from plan so that, for example, project management and the service management organisation can respond accordingly.

Transition plans may require amendment to bring them into line with a reality that has changed since design. This is not the same as bad design or error in selecting transition models, but merely a reflection of a dynamic environment.

## Triggers, inputs, outputs and interfaces

The principal trigger for planning a single transition is the receipt of an authorised change, though longer term planning may be triggered by receipt of a change proposal. Budgeting for future transition requirements will be triggered by the organisation's budgetary planning cycle.

The major input will be a service design package, which includes the release package definition and design specification, test and deployment plans, and service acceptance criteria (SAC).

The outputs will be a transition strategy, budget and an integrated set of service transition plans.

## RELATIONSHIPS WITH OTHER SERVICE MANAGEMENT PROCESSES

Transition planning and support has interfaces to programme and project teams, and customers, as well as to almost every other area of service management including:

- service portfolio management (SPM) and demand management, which should provide long-term information about future proposals and likely resource requirements;
- SPM and business relationship management, to help to manage appropriate two-way communication with customers and strategic planning activities;
- all areas of service design, though this will mainly be through their contribution to the service design package;
- supplier management, to ensure that appropriate contracts are in place;
- other service transition processes that are coordinated by transition planning and support;
- the service operation functions for coordinating pilots, handover and early-life support;
- technical management and application management, which will provide the personnel needed to carry out many aspects of service transition (e.g. to review changes or plan deployments).

The transition planning and support process makes heavy use of the service knowledge management system to provide access to the full range of information needed for short-, medium- and long-range planning.

## METRICS

Every organisation needs to develop its own critical success factors (CSFs) and key performance indicators (KPIs) based on their objectives. Needless to say, they need to be monitored and acted on where necessary. Table 19.1 includes some sample CSFs and a small number of typical KPIs that support the CSFs.

**Table 19.1 Sample critical CSFs and a small number of typical KPIs that support the CSF**

| CSF | KPI |
| --- | --- |
| Balancing cost, quality and time | • Increase in the number of releases implemented that meet the customer's agreed requirements in terms of cost, quality, scope and release schedule (expressed as a percentage of all releases).<br>• Reduced variation of actual versus predicted scope, quality, cost and time. |
| Effective communication with stakeholders | • Increased customer and user satisfaction with plans and communications.<br>• Reduced business disruption due to better alignment between service transition plans and business activities. |
| Identifying and managing risks of failure and disruption | • Reduction in number of issues, risks and delays.<br>• Improved service transition success rates. |
| Coordinating activities of multiple processes involved in each transition | • Improved efficiency and effectiveness, e.g. sharing tool licences.<br>• Reduction in time and resource to develop and maintain integrated plans and coordination activities. |
| Managing conflicting demands for shared resources | • Increased satisfaction with the service transition practices.<br>• Reduced number of issues caused by conflicts. |

# 20  KNOWLEDGE MANAGEMENT

## INTRODUCTION AND SCOPE

The ability to deliver quality services is directly influenced by the people involved in the delivery, especially by their understanding of situations, possible response options, and the consequences and benefits of those options (i.e. by their knowledge). This applies across all phases of the lifecycle.

Incidents which actually relate to a common underlying problem may present themselves with different symptoms. It is unrealistic to expect that all service desk staff will have the same knowledge about the relationship between possible symptoms and the cause, and hence automatically offer a suitable response. Being able to store and correlate information about such things and present the shared knowledge back to the service desk staff will enable them to be more effective.

Typically, knowledge management is displayed within the Data-to-Information-to-Knowledge-to-Wisdom (DIKW) model as illustrated in Figure 20.1 and where the terms are defined as:

- **Data:** Discrete set of facts.
- **Information:** Data set in context.
- **Knowledge:** Uses information, but includes an extra dimension derived from experience.
- **Wisdom:** Uses knowledge to make correct decisions and judgements.

It is unrealistic to expect every individual to have a deep and broad range of knowledge, but it is possible to record, store and make data, information and knowledge available to people.

## PURPOSE AND OBJECTIVES

The purpose of knowledge management is to ensure that the right person has the right knowledge at the right time to enable them to make sensible decisions about courses of action.

**Figure 20.1 The DIKW model**

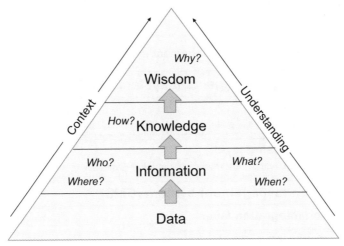

The objectives are to provide:

- more efficient services with improved quality, increased satisfaction and reduced cost;
- a clear and common understanding of the value provided by services and how that value is realised;
- relevant information on usage, resource consumption, constraints and difficulties that is always available.

## KEY ACTIVITIES

The key activities of knowledge management are to gather, analyse, store and share knowledge and information within an organisation. To this end, an organisation needs to implement a service knowledge management system (SKMS), as represented in a basic form in Figure 20.2.

The SKMS is a set of tools and databases that are used to manage knowledge and information. It includes the configuration management system, as well as other tools and databases. The SKMS stores, manages, updates and presents all information that an IT service provider needs to manage the full lifecycle of IT services.

The SKMS is underpinned by the configuration management system (CMS), the configuration management databases (CMDBs) and other service management databases. In its wider context it also holds knowledge from other sources such as:

- the experience of technical staff;
- records of peripheral matters of interest (e.g. weather, user numbers and behaviours, market conditions);

- suppliers and partner requirements, abilities and skills;
- user skill levels (e.g. use of PCs or the internet).

**Figure 20.2 Service knowledge management system**

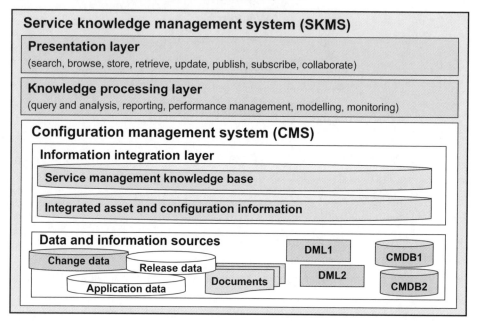

## ACTIVITIES, METHODS AND TECHNIQUES

An overall knowledge management strategy is required, including how to identify, capture and maintain knowledge and the underpinning data. It is also necessary to consider knowledge transfer (i.e. retrieving and sharing knowledge in order to solve problems) and support dynamic learning, strategic planning and decision-making. Evaluation and improvement is important as with other service management processes. We must measure the use made of the data, evaluate its usefulness and identify improvements.

## CHALLENGES

Establishing effective knowledge management can be very challenging. Making incorrect choices in certain areas can lead, at the extremes, to paralysis by data overload or information which is so sparse as to be useless. It is essential that all data sources are trustworthy, accurate and up to date, as is the case for configuration management data. Key aspects are:

- understanding what knowledge is necessary to support the decisions that must be made;

- understanding which conditions need to be monitored (changing external and internal circumstances, ranging from end-user demand, legal requirements through to weather forecasts);

- the cost of capturing and maintaining data, and the value that data may bring, bearing in mind the negative impact of data overload on effective knowledge transfer;

- intellectual property rights and copyright issues;

- ensuring that information is not easily open to misinterpretation.

**EXAMPLE**

In 2011, at a conference of local authorities, the head of a County Council described a situation where a woman reporting the death of her husband had to make more than thirty telephone calls to different Council departments. At this point, the government decreed that in future in that circumstance, the individual would only have to make a single call. However, from a Council perspective, correlating data across different databases is a non-trivial task, either because there is a lack of common data such as National Insurance number or a lack of data integration. Similar situations are extant in banks that have grown by acquisition without integrating customer data across the multiple databases, explaining why when you visit a branch to pay in cash, you may often be asked whether you want a mortgage, loan or credit card, since their systems are often incapable of correlating all the data they have on a particular individual.

## RELATIONSHIPS WITH OTHER SERVICE MANAGEMENT PROCESSES

Almost by definition, knowledge management interfaces with all the other service management processes, but it also interfaces with everyone within the business and suppliers, customers and external sources of information.

## METRICS

The metrics indicating success are found in the wider service management sphere:

- Reduced time and effort required to support and maintain services.

- Reduced time to find information for diagnosing and fixing incidents and problems.

- Changes and releases implemented in timely manner.

- Reduced dependency on personnel for knowledge.

- Fewer errors made because available information was not used.

## ROLES

The knowledge manager's responsibilities include:

- ensuring that the service provider is able to gather, analyse, store and share knowledge and information;
- improving efficiency by reducing the need to rediscover knowledge.

# 21 SERVICE ASSET AND CONFIGURATION MANAGEMENT

## INTRODUCTION AND SCOPE

Organisations invest huge amounts of money in IT equipment and ancillary resources, which are assets of the organisation. Accordingly, we need to maintain information about those assets in terms of their source, value, location, who controls them etc. This is asset management.

Configuration management goes beyond this in providing us with information about the relationships that exist between the various components. This is essential to effective service management solutions since this information underpins all of the other processes particularly incident, problem, availability and change management.

When a change is proposed, comprehensive configuration information enables the rapid and accurate assessment of the impact of the change on services and components. Similarly, calls to the service desk can be simplified if the agent can automatically see what services and systems the caller uses.

## PURPOSE AND OBJECTIVES

The purpose of service asset and configuration management (SACM) is to:

- identify and control all items of interest;
- manage and protect the integrity of assets.

The objectives of SACM is to define and control the components of services and infrastructure, and to maintain accurate configuration information on the historical, current and planned states of these components, services and infrastructure.

Asset management covers service assets across the whole service lifecycle. It provides a complete inventory of assets and records who is responsible for their control. It includes full lifecycle management of IT and service assets, from the point of acquisition through maintenance to disposal.

Configuration management provides a configuration model of the services, assets and infrastructure by recording the relationships between service assets and configuration items. It ensures that components are identified, baselined and maintained and that changes to them are controlled. The scope covers interfaces to internal and external service providers where there are assets and configuration items that need to be controlled (e.g. shared assets).

SACM optimises the performance of service assets and configurations and therefore improves the overall performance of the service and minimises the costs and risks caused by poorly managed assets (e.g. service outages, fines, incorrect licence fees and failed audits).

## BASIC CONCEPTS

All of the information that we are interested in will be held in a repository known as the configuration management system (CMS) as a series of configuration item (CI) records, each of which has descriptive information (known as attributes) including relationship data to other CIs. The CMS will typically consist of one or more configuration management databases (CMDBs). Historically, there has often been confusion about this aspect, with many organisations striving to develop a single physical CMDB when it is the logical concept of a repository, the CMS, which is important.

A configuration item can be anything that is of relevance that needs to be managed in order to provide an IT service, for example hardware, software, people, documentation, infrastructure and the services themselves. They are under change management control.

CIs should be selected using established selection criteria, grouped, classified and identified in such a way that they are manageable and traceable throughout the service lifecycle.

One of the most challenging aspects of establishing effective configuration management is defining the most appropriate level at which CIs are defined. A balance must be struck between having sufficient information to be truly useful and the effort that is involved in collecting and maintaining the information.

Representing the components and their relationships pictorially can help greatly in reaching an understanding of what is required.

Configurations can be modelled to illustrate the relationship between the various CIs to provide a means for assessing the impact of incidents, problems and changes, and for identifying ways of optimisation of assets and managing costs. An example of a configuration model is shown in Figure 21.1.

A configuration management system is more that a simple repository of data and information.

The CMS contains information about the logical software components, while the DML is a secure library which contains the definitive authorised versions of software approved for live use within the organisation, regardless of their source. The CMS and DML are used together in the building of a release prior to deployment, as illustrated in Figure 21.2.

**Figure 21.1 Example of a logical configuration model**

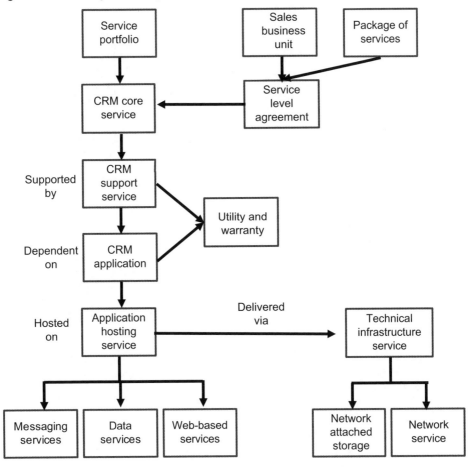

Software held in the DML will have passed quality assurance tests, demonstrating its integrity and its freedom from viruses. DML software can be trusted. As said above, the DML stores definitive versions irrespective of source and essential documentation. It therefore holds not only in-house developed software but also third party/purchased software, along with licence documents or evidence of licences purchased.

The DML must be secure, in terms of preventing unauthorised access, in terms of SACM controlling what comes into and goes out of the store and, critically, in terms of the physical security and safety of its contents in the event of fire, flood and so on.

## CONFIGURATION BASELINE

A configuration baseline is the configuration of a service, product or infrastructure that has been formally reviewed and agreed on, which thereafter serves as the basis for further activities and can be changed only through formal change procedures. A configuration

**Figure 21.2 Relationship between the DML and the CMS**

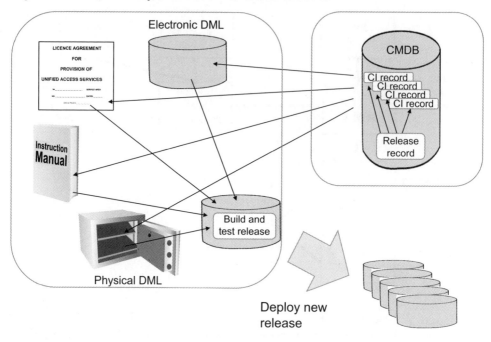

baseline can be used to checkpoint a service development milestone, as a basis for future builds and changes, to assemble components for a change or release and to provide the basis for a configuration audit or back-out.

## ACTIVITIES

The key activities of SACM are illustrated in Figure 21.3 and are:

- **management and planning:** defining the level of configuration management required for a service or a change project;

- **configuration identification:** defining CI types and groupings, naming conventions etc.;

- **configuration control:** ensuring there are adequate mechanisms to control CIs while maintaining a record of all changes to ensure no mismatch with the physical world;

- **status accounting and reporting:** maintaining the status of CIs as they progress through their discrete states (e.g. development, approved, live, withdrawn);

- **verification and audit:** checking that the physical CIs exist, records in the CMS match the real world and that documentation is accurate;

- **information management:** back-up copies of the CMS should be taken regularly and securely stored. It is advisable for one copy to be stored at a remote location for use in the event of a disaster.

## Figure 21.3 Configuration activities

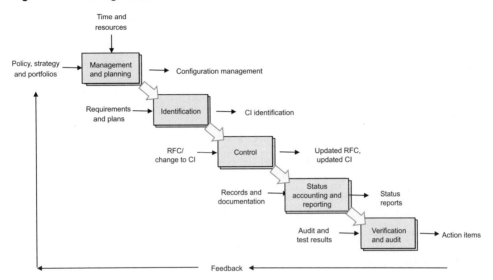

## CHALLENGES

Service asset and configuration management can be one of the most difficult disciplines to introduce. Although it underpins virtually every aspect of service management, it is perceived as having little direct value itself. The following challenges are very common:

- Persuading technical support staff of the value of SACM because they may see it as a hindrance.
- Funding of SACM, because it is not visible to the business.
- Over-engineering and collecting too much data: getting the balance between what can be recorded and what needs to be.
- The CMS can become out of date as CIs are moved or changes are made. An out-of-date CMS is actually very dangerous since incorrect decisions can be made on the basis of the information.

## RELATIONSHIPS WITH OTHER SERVICE MANAGEMENT PROCESSES

SACM underpins virtually every other service management process as we have already seen. The most significant relationships are:

- Change management: identifying the impact of proposed changes;
- Financial management: capturing key financial information;
- IT service continuity management: providing awareness of assets the business depends on and controlling key spare assets and software;

- Incident and problem management: providing and maintaining key diagnostic information and maintaining and providing data to the service desk;
- Availability management: supporting detection of points of failure.

## METRICS

Most of the metrics that indicate successful configuration management are actually seen in other processes. Some of the key ones are:

- the ratio of used licences to paid for licences (this should be close to 1 : 1);
- accuracy in budgets and charges for the assets used by each customer or business unit;
- the percentage reduction in business impact of outages and incidents caused by poor asset and configuration management;
- the reduction in the use of unauthorised hardware and software, and in non-standard and variant builds that increase complexity, support costs and risk to the business services.

## ROLES

- Service asset manager: manages the lifecycle of assets.
- Configuration manager: manages the lifecycle and relationships of all CIs.
- Configuration analyst: analyses/proposes scope of asset and configuration processes; undertakes process activities.
- Configuration administrator/librarian: controls the receipt, identification, storage and withdrawal of all supported CIs (content control).
- CMS/Tools administrator: monitors the performance and capacity of asset and configuration management systems and recommends improvement opportunities (technical control).

# 22   CHANGE MANAGEMENT

## INTRODUCTION AND SCOPE

It is often said that the only constant is change. Accordingly, change must be embraced as an essential and natural aspect of any environment, but poorly managed changes can cause chaos within an organisation. Indeed, poorly managed changes are often the major cause of incidents. Not only does this cause disruption to the users, it also leads to rework that is frequently more difficult to achieve than getting it correct originally.

### EXAMPLE

A major airline suffered several days of upheaval and embarrassment after their reservation system crashed and customers were unable to execute many transactions. The cause was traced to an inadequately tested change to the system. The loss, both financial and reputational, was substantial.

However, a change management process should not be viewed as a bureaucratic inhibitor that makes changes difficult to introduce. Rather it should be an enabler to allow the right changes to proceed as smoothly as possible regardless of their scale or complexity.

Historically, many organisations have had change control mechanisms in place, but these have often been fragmented and divergent in aspects such as assessment and authorisation. To be truly effective, a common, holistic approach to handling change is required.

## PURPOSE AND OBJECTIVES

Change management ensures that IT and the business can be aligned and can be kept aligned with optimal efficiency and minimal disruption, re-work and risk by means of the consistent and effective management of the necessary changes needed to maintain alignment.

The purpose of the change management process is to ensure that all changes are managed through standard methods and procedures that ensure changes are effective, on time, meet their specified requirements and are properly recorded in the configuration management system.

The objective of change management is to ensure that all changes are recorded and then evaluated, authorised, prioritised, planned, tested, implemented, documented and reviewed in a controlled manner.

The scope of change management covers changes to service assets and configuration items across the whole service lifecycle. The process addresses all changes at all levels: strategic, tactical and operational. Hence, although change management is described in the service transition volume, many changes will occur at an operational level and be relatively small in nature.

Organisations can choose whether requests are raised by specific roles or groups only, or whether anyone within the organisation can do so.

## BASIC CONCEPTS

A change request is a formal communication requesting a change to one or more CIs. Different types of change may require different types of change request, each with specific forms and procedures (e.g. for impact assessment and change authorisation). The change types are shown in the Table 22.1.

**Table 22.1  Example types of request by service lifecycle stage**

| Types of change | Procedures | SS | SD | ST | SO | CSI |
|---|---|---|---|---|---|---|
| Service portfolio change:<br>  New portfolio item<br>  Scope, business case or baseline changes<br>  Pipeline | Change management | ✓ | | | | |
| Service or service definition change:<br>  To existing or planned attributes<br>  Service design<br>  Service improvement | Change management | ✓ | ✓ | ✓ | ✓ | ✓ |

*(Continued)*

**Table 22.1 (Continued)**

| Types of change | Procedures | SS | SD | ST | SO | CSI |
|---|---|---|---|---|---|---|
| Project proposal:<br>Business change<br>No impact on service or design baseline | Project change management procedure | ✓ | ✓ | | | ✓ |
| User access request | User access procedure | | | | ✓ | |
| Operational activity:<br>Tuning<br>H/W reboot<br>Planned maintenance | Local procedure | | | | ✓ | |

A request for change (RFC) is a formal request for a change which may be submitted via a paper form or electronically through a service management tool. Most tools will ensure that complete information is provided and automatically add some data such as identifiers and dates. This will avoid wasted time.

Changes are categorised into the following change types:

- **Normal:** Any change that is neither standard nor emergency, that is a change that goes through the full assessment, authorisation and implementation stages.

- **Standard:** Any change that is neither standard nor emergency, that is a pre-approved change that is low risk, relatively common and follows a procedure or work instruction (e.g. a password reset or the provision of a standard PC to a new employee). RFCs are not always required to implement a standard change and they may be logged and tracked using a different mechanism (e.g. through the request fulfilment process). Often operational maintenance changes are treated as standard changes.

- **Emergency:** Reserved only for critical changes that must be introduced as soon as possible (e.g. changes needed to restore failed high-availability services or widespread service failure, or changes that will prevent such a failure from imminently occurring). The change management process normally has a specific procedure for handling emergency changes.

The change authority is the person or persons who will authorise specific changes to take place. Organisations can decide who will be responsible for authorising different types of change and, in the interests of operational efficiency, will often devolve this authority to the change management team or operational staff. It is vital that the designated change authority has the appropriate knowledge and skills to be able to make such decisions. Modern tools will allow electronic approvals, with definable defaults that ensure changes are progressed in a timely manner.

The change advisory board (CAB) is a group of people that advises the change manager in the assessment, prioritisation and scheduling of changes. The CAB is made up of representatives from all relevant areas within the IT service provider, the business and third parties. The key factor is that all parties who have a view on a particular change should be represented. Membership of the CAB is therefore likely to be dynamic, even within a single meeting.

Meetings may involve face-to-face contact or be conducted by telephone or online. Depending on choices made within the organisation, meetings may be held at different times and intervals as demand dictates. CAB members assess both business and technical perspectives of proposed changes.

For emergency changes there may not be time to convene the full CAB, so it is necessary to identify a smaller group with authority to make emergency decisions (i.e. an emergency change advisory board (ECAB)).

Change policy should specify how the composition of the CAB and ECAB will be determined in each instance.

No change should be approved without there being a remediation plan (i.e. what to do if the change is unsuccessful). Where possible, a back-out plan should be provided to recover the organisation to its original, or another, known state should the change fail. This might involve reloading a baselined set of configuration items, revisiting the change itself or, if the failure is severe, invoking the organisation's business continuity plan. It should be recognised that not all changes can be backed out, so the remediation plan must cover what to do in such situations. Only by considering the remediation options available prior to instigating a change and establishing that the remediation is viable, can the risk of the proposed change be determined and the appropriate decisions taken.

The change schedule lists all approved changes and planned implementation dates. It becomes an important audit trail to support incident/problem management among other processes.

A change model is a repeatable way of dealing with a particular type of change. It sets out specific defined steps that are followed for a specific type of change. Standard and emergency changes are typical examples that might be handled this way. Support tools can be used to automate the handling, management, reporting and escalation of the process. The change model includes:

- steps to handle the change including handling issues and unexpected events;

- the chronological order to take the steps, with any dependences or co-processing defined;

- responsibilities (who should do what);
- timescales and thresholds for completion of the actions;
- escalation procedures (who should be contacted and when).

A change model is therefore simply a defined procedure for handling a certain type of change.

## ACTIVITIES

The key activities of change management as a discipline are:

- planning and controlling change;
- understanding the impact of change;
- change decision-making and change authorisation;
- change and release scheduling;
- communication with stakeholders;
- ensuring that there are remediation plans;
- measurement and control;
- management reporting;
- continual improvement.

Figure 22.1 illustrates the process flow of a normal change.

Typical activities in managing individual changes are:

- to create and record the RFC: the change is raised by the individual or organisational group that requires the change;
- to assess and evaluate the change:

  - to establish who should be involved in the assessment and authorisation;
  - to assess and evaluate the business justification, impact, cost, benefits and risk of changes.

- to authorise the change if appropriate;
- to communicate the decision to all stakeholders, in particular the initiator of the RFC;
- to coordinate change implementation;
- to review (i.e. evaluate the success or otherwise of the change and any lessons learned) and close the RFC.

It is important to ensure an accurate impact assessment is completed and that the balance of risk and benefit to the live service is well understood. Without this information,

**Figure 22.1 Example of a process flow for a normal change**

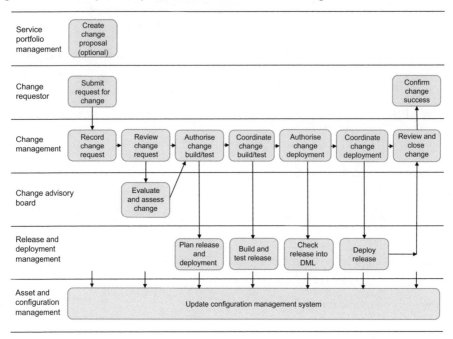

the change may fail to deliver all the possible or expected business benefits or have an unexpected, detrimental effect on the live service. Examples abound of operations teams implementing a change to the underlying infrastructure at the same time that a change is made to an application; usually with catastrophic results.

## CHANGE PROPOSALS

To properly manage major changes, such as the introduction of a new or changed service, change proposals are submitted to change management to avoid potential issues such as negative impacts on live services or excessive or conflicting resource demands. If the change proposal is authorised, it allows the service to be chartered and the service design activity to be initiated. However, this is not authorisation of the change itself.

The change proposal usually comes from the service portfolio management process and should include:

- a high-level description of the change;
- a business case;
- a timeline for the change.

If change management authorises the change proposal, then it is included in the change schedule. Subsequent RFCs should cross-reference the change proposal.

## CHALLENGES

In trying to establish effective change management, the following challenges are commonly encountered:

- Inaccurate configuration details leading to poor evaluation and higher risk of change failure.
- The process is defined in, or perceived as, an over-bureaucratic way that hinders effective operation of IT and its services.
- People bypass the process (especially if it is seen to be bureaucratic).
- Too many changes are treated as emergencies.
- Accountability for changes isn't clearly defined leading to poor quality and compliance.
- Striking the right balance between stable production and being responsive to business needs.

## TESTING

All changes should be tested and it is worth pointing out that change testing is primarily the subject of the service validation and testing process and to a lesser extent the change evaluation process, neither of which is covered in this book because they are outside the foundation syllabus.

## RELATIONSHIPS WITH OTHER SERVICE MANAGEMENT PROCESSES

Interfaces with change management include:

### Organisational level processes

- Integration with business change processes to ensure change issues, aims and impacts are exchanged.
- Programme and project management need to align to change.
- Sourcing and partnering require effective change management to manage relationships.

### Asset and configuration management

- Enables change impact assessment and tracking of change workflow.
- CMS may identify related CIs affected by a change but not included in the original request.

### Problem management

- Changes are often required to implement workaround and fix known errors.

## IT service continuity management

- IT service continuity plans need to be updated via change management.

## Information security management

- Changes required by security are under change management.

## Capacity and demand management

- Capacity management needs to assess impact of changes on capacity.
- Changes required by capacity management are under change management.

## Service portfolio management

Change proposals for major changes, such as new or changed services, are usually created by the service portfolio management process.

## METRICS

These are the measures that indicate successful, or at least improving, change management:

- Increasing number of implemented changes meeting the customer's agreed requirements.
- A reduction in the number of disruptions to services, defects and rework caused by 'poor' changes.
- A reduction in the number of unauthorised changes.
- A reduction in the number and percentage of unplanned changes and emergency fixes.
- An increasing change success rate (percentage of changes deemed successful at review/number of RFCs approved).
- A reduction in the percentage of incidents attributable to changes.

## ROLES

The prime role is that of the change manager, whose responsibilities include:

- managing the quality, review, assessment and approval of RFCs;
- chairing the CAB;
- acting as key liaison between initiators and approvers of changes.

# 23 RELEASE AND DEPLOYMENT MANAGEMENT

## INTRODUCTION AND SCOPE

Once a new or changed service has been developed, we need to get it into the live environment, activate it and provide support while it beds down. Most commonly, people think about releasing new versions of software, but the concept applies equally to hardware and other components such as documentation. Indeed, major upgrades or new services will frequently involve combinations of all elements.

In the past, many issues were caused by development simply passing control to operations in a 'clean-break' move. Release and deployment management is concerned with making this a more phased and controlled process, including a period of early life support to ensure that everything is working as it should and can be used by the business.

Effective release and deployment processes require close interaction between development and operations, preventing the 'throwing it over the wall' syndrome so prevalent in the past.

## PURPOSE AND OBJECTIVES

There must be clear plans that enable the business to align its activities with them and everyone must be satisfied with the mechanisms used.

Release and deployment management aims to build, test and deliver new or changed services successfully into the production environment within required timescales and with minimal disruption to existing services.

The purpose is to ensure that consistent and integral release packages are deployed in line with agreed policy and with plans agreed with the customers and stakeholders, and that this takes place under full and effective control. Any associated business and business process changes, including training and skills transfer, must be managed to take place in a timescale that is aligned with the release timetable.

The objective is to ensure that there are clear consistent plans that everyone understands and follows, that releases are managed efficiently and effectively through to deployment and use and that the new service and supporting systems are capable of being operated successfully and deliver the agreed service requirements (utility and warranty).

The scope of release and deployment management includes the processes, systems and functions required to package, build, test and deploy a release into production in accordance with the service design package (SDP). This includes handover to the service operation lifecycle stage.

Effective release and deployment management adds value by ensuring that customers and users can use the new or changed service in a way that supports the business, and by delivering change faster and at optimum cost and minimal risk. Well-planned and well-implemented release and deployment can make a significant difference to an organisation's service costs by minimising troubleshooting and rework.

## BASIC CONCEPTS

The two constituent aspects of the process are release and deployment.

A release is a construct of one or more changes to one or more components of an IT service that have been built, tested and will be deployed together. Deployment is the process of implementing the release in the live environment.

A key concept is that of a release unit (i.e. the components of a service that are normally released together). A release unit typically includes sufficient components to perform a useful function. For example, one release unit might be a desktop PC, including hardware, software, licences, documentation etc. There might be standardised units for different roles or departments, or the desktop might be customised for each new recruit (where each instance is a separate release unit). Another release unit might be a complete application, including IT operations procedures and user training.

It is possible that a release will consist of more than one release unit. A release package is one or more release units that are required to implement a new or changed service.

A release policy should be defined as part of the management control over releases. In fact, it is unlikely that an organisation will have a single release policy; it is more likely to have several, each covering one or more services. Each policy should cover identification, roles and responsibilities, expected frequency, change acceptance criteria, automation, configuration verification, entry and exit criteria through phases, and handover from early life support to operations.

## ACTIVITIES, METHODS AND TECHNIQUES

Figure 23.1 shows the four basic steps or phases in the release and deployment process.

- **Release and deployment planning:** Commenced once change management authorises the planning of a release.
- **Release build and test:**

  - The release package is built and tested.
  - The release package is checked into the definitive media library (DML) in readiness for deployment into the live environment.

- **Deployment:** The release package is deployed from the DML into the live environment.

- **Review and close:** Did the release perform as expected and meet the anticipated requirements?

Whether a single RFC is required for the whole deployment process or a separate RFC for each step in the process is at the discretion of each organisation.

**Figure 23.1  Basic release and deployment process steps**

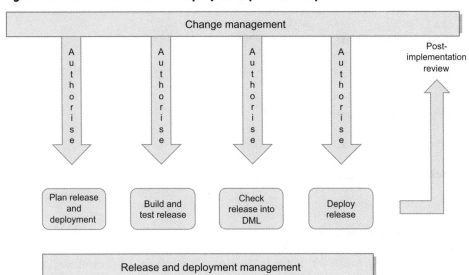

## CHALLENGES

The challenges that organisations will face when defining the right policies and implementing effective release and deployment include:

- striking the right balance between flexibility and stability in the release policy – too much flexibility can introduce instability, too little flexibility can fail to meet the needs of stakeholders;

- establishing standard performance metrics for all transitions;

- dealing with inaccurate project or supplier delivery dates;

- understanding all the stakeholder perspectives;

- understanding the risks;

- taking a pragmatic approach to the challenges of delivery.

## RELATIONSHIPS WITH OTHER SERVICE MANAGEMENT PROCESSES

The key interfaces include:

### Change management

All releases are driven by an authorised RFC.

### Service asset and configuration management

Providing input for the components during the build and updating during the various phases of the release and deployment.

### Incident management

Particularly during early life support when extra attention and resources may be required.

### IT service continuity management

Continuity plans must be updated to reflect the new or changed service.

### Capacity management

New resources may be required or loads on existing ones changed.

### Service design coordination

Release and deployment contributes to the creation of the service design package and ultimately uses this as a key input to the release and deployment activities.

### Transition planning and support

Provides a release and deployment framework and context, and helps support multiple concurrent releases.

## METRICS

The following are some of the metrics for assessing the effectiveness of the process:

- The variance in service performance against that required by customers (should be minimal and reducing).
- The number of incidents recorded against the service (should be low and reducing).
- Increased customer and user satisfaction with the services delivered.

- Reduced customer dissatisfaction caused by poorly tested and deployed services.
- Reduced incidents and problems in deployment and production.
- Reduced discrepancies between the registered data in the CMS and the real world.

## ROLES

The release packaging and design manager's responsibilities include:

- establishing the final release configuration and building the final release;
- testing the release and publishing known errors and workarounds.

The deployment manager's responsibilities include:

- planning, scheduling and controlling the movement of releases to test in live environments;
- ensuring that the integrity of the live environment is protected and that the correct components are released.

# 24  THE SERVICE DESK

## INTRODUCTION AND SCOPE

The service desk is a function and not a process. A function is a defined group of people who carry out a process or processes. The service desk typically conducts a number of processes, in particular incident management and request fulfilment.

The service desk is made up of a group of staff trained to deal with service events. Service desk staff will have access to the necessary tools to manage these events.

For most IT users within an organisation, the service desk will be their only contact with the IT Department. Therefore, the impression made by the service desk in the handling of events will have a large influence on how the IT Department as a whole is viewed within that organisation.

The service desk should be the single point of contact for IT users within an organisation. The size and structure of a service desk will be driven by the size and structure of the organisation it supports. The number and skills of the IT user community and their geographical spread are factors.

The service desk is the single point of contact for all IT users wishing to log an incident, report an event, initiate a change request, make a service request or raise a query regarding any of the services that the IT Department provides.

## PURPOSE AND OBJECTIVES

The main objectives of the service desk are to restore service as quickly as possible (incident management) following a failure and to fulfil service requests efficiently and effectively (request fulfilment).

## BASIC CONCEPTS

### Methods of contacting the service desk

Traditionally, most IT users have contacted their service desk via telephone. However, there are various methods of making contact with a service desk:

- Telephone;
- Web interface;

148

- Automated alert;
- Email;
- Pager;
- Personal contact.

## Single point of contact

It is very important that the service desk is the single point of contact for IT users within an organisation. Without a single point of contact, there is no control and ownership throughout the management of incidents, service requests and queries.

It is the service desk which owns incidents throughout their lifecycle. It does not matter who is working on the incident, the ownership remains with the service desk. The service desk will receive and log incidents or service request details. They will undertake first-line investigation and diagnosis with escalation if incidents or service requests are not resolved.

The existence of the single point of contact can be reinforced by advertising the sole service desk number and/or email address as widely as possible.

## Service Desk structures

The service desk can be structured in a number of ways. The structure should be driven by the nature of the business supported. Factors such as user skill profile and geographical location of users will influence the structure.

Service desk structures are defined below.

**Local service desk:** Local service desks (Figure 24.1) are situated adjacent to the users that they support. Frequently, this means that they are in the same building or on the same site as the people who contact them.

---

**Figure 24.1 Local service desk**

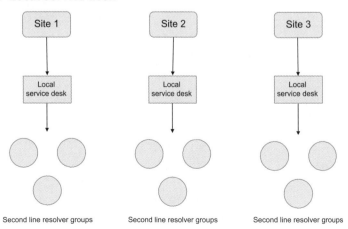

The advantages of such a structure are visibility of the service desk function and easy communication links. However, there are disadvantages such as the risk of incidents not being prioritised in line with business impact because users are able to physically visit the service desk and request/demand action. Another potential disadvantage is that service desk staff are not used as efficiently as they would be under other service desk structures because they are 'fixed' in one place supporting local users.

Good reasons for adopting a local service desk structure include time zone restrictions, language issues, the requirement to support a specialist group of users needing specialist support or the requirement to support specific services which again require specialist support. There may even be arguments for having a local service desk adjacent to and available to key users. Such key users may be important functionally, in that they undertake processes critical to the business of the organisation or hierarchically in that are at a senior level. (N.B. seniority should not drive the prioritisation of an incident. Incidents should always be prioritised on the basis of business impact and urgency.)

**Centralised service desk:** Typically, organisations have moved away from local service desks to adopting a centralised service desk (Figure 24.2). Efficiency and cost-effectiveness are the reasons for this. Economies of scale can be exploited by having all of the organisation's service desk staff in one physical location. By adopting a single telephone number, calls from anywhere in the organisation will be directed to the centralised service desk. It should not matter to the user where their call is dealt with; their only interest ought to be the way in which the call is handled.

One of the few disadvantages of a centralised service desk is that there is no default contingency plan should the service desk become inaccessible.

---

**Figure 24.2  Centralised service desk**

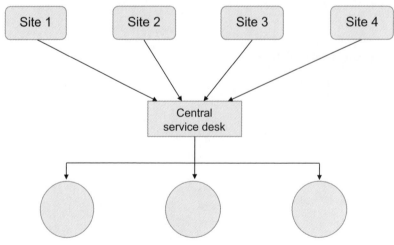

Second line resolver groups

**Virtual service desk:** From the user's point of view, the response they receive from a virtual service desk (Figure 24.3) will be the same as the one they receive from a centralised service desk. However, the persons who operate a virtual service desk can be in a number of different locations. By utilising a single universal tool, users are able to obtain a service which is the same regardless of their location or the location of the responding service desk staff.

One advantage of such a structure is that it allows far greater staff flexibility. Staff may be able to work from home or organisations may be able to be more efficient by using offshore working by some or all of the service desk staff. There is, however, a risk that service quality lacks consistency and this is something that needs to be managed via metrics designed to measure the quality of service from the various locations.

**Follow the sun:** Organisations with sites around the world may find it more efficient to switch between two or three service desks during a 24-hour period. For example, the service desk based in Singapore would take all the incoming calls for eight hours prior to switching to the Madrid service desk. Madrid would be the service desk through normal European working hours before switching to Chicago. After another eight hours, Chicago would switch back to Singapore and so on.

The advantage of this approach is that it makes it possible for service desk staff to work a normal shift without the need for overtime and additional payments.

**Figure 24.3 Virtual service desk**

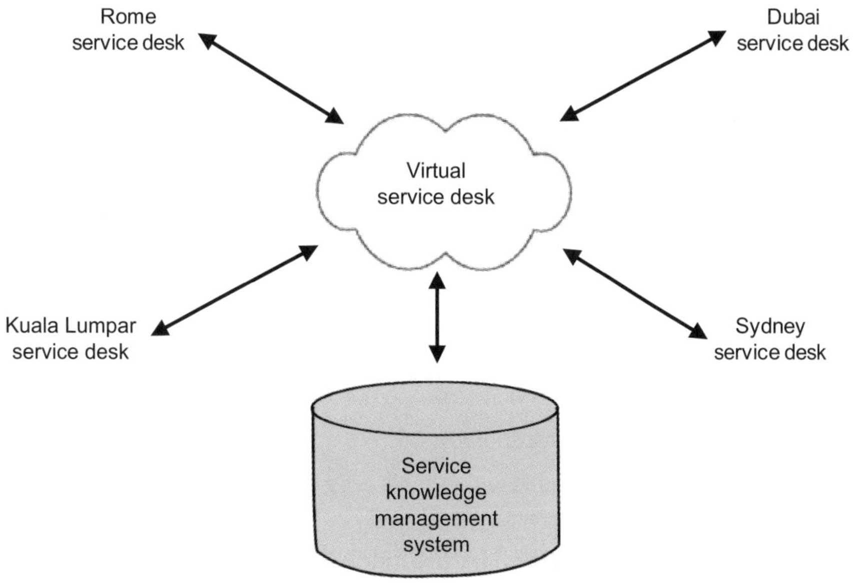

A 'follow the sun' approach relies on good handovers between the sites. Language can be an issue and it is crucial that information from users is recorded in a central tool in such a way that it is understood wherever it is picked up.

**Specialised service desk groups:** Within service desks it is possible to put together specialist groups who perhaps look after one particular high profile or complex service. Where this happens, calls can be routed to the specialist group via the telephony with an option being given to the caller to divert to the group.

## KEY ACTIVITIES

The key activity undertaken by the service desk is to manage incidents, events and service requests as effectively and as efficiently as possible. In order to facilitate this, service desk staff need to have certain skills. It is the application of these skills, along with the use of an appropriate toolset, that allows the service desk to be effective and efficient.

### Skills required by service desk staff

Staff should be recruited with the skills listed below. Ongoing training is required to ensure that these skills are being translated into an effective service and to ensure that the quality of that service is consistent. Service desk staff should be:

- customer focused;
- business aware;
- service aware;
- technology aware;
- articulate.

They should have:

- good interpersonal skills;
- the ability to translate the user description into an incident narrative.

Training will be needed on:

- the processes used by the service desk;
- using the tool and relevant technology;
- problem-solving skills (if this is within their scope).

## RELATIONSHIPS WITH SERVICE MANAGEMENT PROCESSES

The service desk undertakes a number of service management processes, primarily incident management and request fulfilment. There will also be links to many other processes. Service level management provides the targets for incident and request handling. Change management will provide details of forthcoming changes allowing the service desk to plan, train and roster staff accordingly.

## METRICS

Metrics should be put in place to measure the performance of the service desk. While call volumes are important to indicate required staffing levels, they are not a measure of service desk performance or something that the service desk can necessarily control.

Metrics include:

- the average time to resolve an incident (where the incident is resolved by the service desk and not subject to functional escalation);
- the percentage of calls resolved by the service desk;
- the average time to escalate an incident (this can then be compared with the relevant SLA);
- the average cost of calls (calls will be different, but this figure is useful for planning and assessing long-term trends).

## ROLES

There are potentially a number of roles to be fulfilled on a service desk. These include:

- service desk manager;
- service desk supervisor;
- service desk analyst;
- super user (normally located at a user site rather than with the service desk).

The mix of roles will be determined by the size of the organisation being supported and the type of support being provided.

## CHALLENGES

Challenges facing service desks include:

- recruiting, training and retaining staff with the appropriate skills;
- procuring, utilising and maximising the performance of an appropriate service desk tool;
- ensuring that the service desk is the single point of contact;
- ensuring that the service desk is not bypassed;
- obtaining meaningful customer satisfaction data.

# 25  REQUEST FULFILMENT

## INTRODUCTION AND SCOPE

Request fulfilment is the process that carries out service requests from users. From a service desk point of view, the process of request fulfilment tends to cover all the calls that are not incidents. It covers standard change requests, requests for information and complaints. Password resets and queries about obtaining additional software are some of the higher volume requests.

Requests are usually high in volume, but low risk and low cost. A separate distinct process is in place to avoid confusion with the incident handling that the service desk is also undertaking.

Standard changes are relatively commonly occurring ones that are low risk and can be submitted and managed using a predefined procedure or work instruction.

## PURPOSE AND OBJECTIVES

The objective of the process is to manage the service requests effectively and efficiently. Request fulfilment allows users to obtain information and complete standard changes within agreed service levels.

## KEY ACTIVITIES

Request fulfilment should be made as simple as possible. Unlike incidents, requests ought to be predictable and planned for. It will depend on the size and scale of an organisation whether requests are handled through the same logging procedure as incidents. For organisations with a large number of requests, a separate logging and progressing procedure may be appropriate.

The key role of request fulfilment is to handle a large number of requests efficiently and to avoid any bureaucratic bottlenecks. Users will be frustrated if a legitimate request or query cannot be efficiently managed. A holistic view of the situation can be taken by handling all the requests in one place, allowing training needs, communication gaps and requirements for standard changes to be identified.

## REQUEST MODELS

Where high volumes of the same or similar requests are expected, a process model can be defined to standardise the activities to be undertaken. Adoption of request models will streamline the process and allow greater volumes to be processed.

## RELATIONSHIPS WITH OTHER SERVICE MANAGEMENT PROCESSES

### Financial management

There needs to be a strong link between financial management and request fulfilment to ensure that volumes, workload and use of resources are fully understood.

### Change management

Where the request model relates to a standard change, there will have been the necessary review from change management, which may have taken into consideration the relevant financial aspects.

# 26 INCIDENT MANAGEMENT

## INTRODUCTION AND SCOPE

Incident management is the process for dealing with all incidents. These may be incidents where service is being disrupted or incidents where service has not yet been disrupted.

The value of incident management to the business is that resources are allocated to minimising and mitigating the impact of incidents and service unavailability in line with business priorities. Lower levels of incidents and quicker resolution times will enable the services to run as intended.

During the handling of incidents, the service desk may be able to identify improvements in both business and technical processes. The service desk often has a unique position within organisations in that its staff can take a holistic view of how the organisation operates, allowing good practice to be propagated and bad practice to be eradicated.

## PURPOSE AND OBJECTIVES

The main objective of the incident management process is to restore normal service operation as quickly as possible and to minimise the adverse impact on business operations.

## BASIC CONCEPTS

Any unplanned interruption to a service, a degradation in the quality of a particular service or even a failure of a configuration item that has not yet degraded service are considered to be incidents.

- **Timescales:** Timescales for incident handling and triggers for escalation should be agreed and documented in the SLA. Performance against SLA can then be measured and reported. Tools can be configured to enable automated escalation in accordance with the agreed timescales.

- **Incident models:** The adoption of incident models is a method of standardising and automating, if possible, the approach to groups of similar incidents. An incident model is a defined set of steps to be undertaken. Incident model details can be input into the incident handling tool(s).

- **Major incidents:** A major incident is usually defined as an incident with either the highest priority or the highest impact, however different organisations will have different definitions for what constitutes a major incident. For some organisations, the trigger for 'calling' a major incident is when a certain number of users have been impacted. For other organisations, the trigger may be the actual or potential financial loss from the loss of service. If the actual or potential financial loss is over a certain amount, the incident becomes major. For some business areas in some industries, there may be risk of injury or loss of life if particular services are not available. Again, this may be the trigger for the incident becoming major. Reputational damage to the organisation can be another trigger.

Larger organisations may have dedicated major incident management teams available 24/7 who take control of incidents that have been designated major. One of the important roles that major incident managers undertake is to protect those (frequently IT operations management, technical management and application management staff) who are trying to restore service from the communication demands being made on them. During a major incident, there will be many demands and requests for updates which need to be managed. Major incident management teams will have established routes for communication and escalation (both functional and hierarchical).

Major incidents are usually handled in a similar way to other incidents but are progressed with great urgency and with higher profile within the organisation. Activities undertaken must still be logged, but the focus is on restoring the service as quickly as possible with the minimum of disruption.

## KEY ACTIVITIES

### Incident management process flow

The incident management process flow is illustrated in Figure 26.1 and contains the following steps:

- **Inputs to the process:** Incidents can be detected and reported in various ways. Users will call the service desk to report incidents. Technical staff may log incidents or email details of an incident they have identified to the service desk. Increasingly incidents are raised via web interfaces. The event management process will also report incidents by monitoring.

- **Incident identification:** Work to understand and resolve incidents cannot start until an incident has been identified. For this reason, monitoring of the components that make up key services is essential. Incidents can be identified in various ways by users, technical staff and by monitoring.

- **Incident logging:** All incidents should be logged with the date and time being recorded. At this stage, the information required to manage the incident will be logged. This will include a unique reference number, a description of symptoms, the service or CI impacted, the impact, its urgency and the name of the person raising the incident or the method of raising the incident.

# Figure 26.1 Incident management process flow

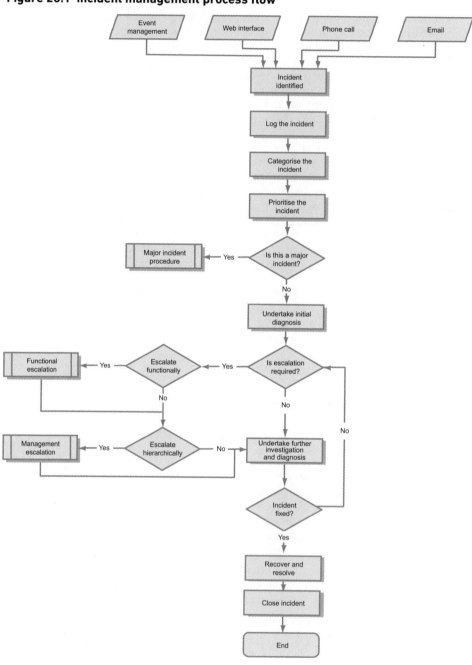

- **Incident categorisation:** A suitable categorisation code will be allocated. For example, this may be hardware or software with sub-codes for lower level categorisation. Accurate categorisation is important because it will allow useful metrics to be gathered highlighting areas of the infrastructure where incidents are occurring. This information is typically used by problem management.

- **Incident prioritisation:** The priority of an incident is based on the impact and the urgency. Impact is the 'pain' to the business. Impact may relate to the number of users impacted, the potential financial loss to the organisation, the risk of breach of regulatory or legislative rules or, for some services, the risk of loss of life. Urgency relates to how quickly the business requires the incident to be resolved.

Table 26.1 illustrates a simplistic priority coding system.

**Table 26.1 A simplistic incident priority coding system**

|  |  | Impact | | |
| --- | --- | --- | --- | --- |
|  |  | High | Medium | Low |
|  | High | Priority 1 | Priority 2 | Priority 3 |
| **Urgency** | Medium | Priority 2 | Priority 3 | Priority 4 |
|  | Low | Priority 3 | Priority 4 | Priority 5 |

Target resolution times will have been allocated to each priority level. These will have been agreed with the business and recorded in the SLA.

- **Initial diagnosis:** If the incident has been raised by a call to the service desk, then it will be the service desk which conducts the initial diagnosis, usually while the user is still on the telephone. The availability of diagnostic scripts will help as will the ability to match against problems and known errors. The CMDB may also be consulted at this stage.

- **Incident escalation:** Escalation may be functional or hierarchical.

  - Functional escalation occurs when the service desk is not able to resolve the incident or where the incident has not been resolved within the target resolution time. The service desk will involve second-level support, which has more specific technical knowledge. Further functional escalation may occur through the lifecycle of the incident to third-level support, which may be part of the organisation or third parties such as suppliers. It is important to remember that the ownership of an incident always remains with the service desk regardless of which other support areas are working on a resolution.

- Hierarchical escalation raises the profile of a specific incident within the IT organisation and also within business areas. More senior IT staff are able to provide focus and resources, but ownership of the incident will be retained by the service desk. Organisations will have triggers that indicate when hierarchical escalation is required. This may be for all 'priority 1' incidents or when incidents of a certain priority have not been resolved with a target timescale. The triggers for escalation will be recorded in the relevant SLA and ought to be highlighted by the support tool in use. The service desk will keep the user informed of all functional or hierarchical escalations that occur during the lifecycle of an incident and at the same time the incident record will be updated.

- **Investigation and diagnosis:** In this phase of the incident lifecycle, work is undertaken by the service desk or support areas to understand what has to be done in order to restore service. This is often the most time-consuming part of the process although it can be speeded up using diagnostic scripts and by reference to other incidents and problems as well as known error databases.

- **Resolution and recovery:** The investigation and diagnosis phase will arrive at a resolution. This needs to be applied and then testing needs to take place to ensure that the incident has been resolved and service restored. There may be a time lag between a fix being applied and the service running normally again (e.g. there may be a backlog of processing to catch up on). On other occasions, it may not be possible to ascertain whether the fix has worked for a period of time (e.g. if the original issue was with a month-end process). Regardless of where the resolution has been put in place or who was involved, the incident should be passed back to the service desk for closure.

- **Incident closure:** Only the service desk should close incidents. It needs the user's agreement that the incident has been resolved. All incident documentation will have to be completed prior to closure and a closure category allocated to allow meaningful metrics to be produced. User satisfaction surveys ought to be conducted for an agreed (in the SLA) percentage of incidents. These user satisfaction surveys can be undertaken via telephone, email or web interface.

## RELATIONSHIPS WITH OTHER SERVICE MANAGEMENT PROCESSES

Incident management is closely linked to problem management with one or more incidents being caused by a problem. There is also a strong link with change management. Changes are often implemented to resolve an incident or a number of incidents and, unfortunately, changes that do not do exactly what they were intended to do may cause incidents. Service asset and configuration management provides the information needed to manage incidents. Service level management will provide the target resolution times together with escalation criteria. Incident management is also instrumental in supporting service level agreements.

## METRICS

Useful incident metrics include:

- the percentage of incidents resolved within SLA;
- the average cost of an incident;
- the average cost of a major incident;
- the percentage of incidents that are major.

Additionally, from a staffing point of view, it is important to know the volume of both incidents and major incidents. On their own, these metrics do not necessarily give a measure of effectiveness or efficiency, but they are important in understanding the scale of the issues being raised.

## ROLES

The incident management process owner will write the incident management policy, which will include procedures and metrics to ensure that wherever the process is carried out, it is done so in a consistent manner.

The incident manager is responsible for the effectiveness and efficiency of the incident management process. First-line support is conducted by the service desk with second- and third-line support being provided by technical teams either internal to the organisation or via third parties.

## CHALLENGES

### Difference between incident and problem management

There is a very real difference between incident management and problem management. Incident management is solely focused on restoring service as quickly as possible while problem management's aim is to understand and tackle the root cause. This can lead to tension between the two processes.

### Other challenges

- Early detection of incidents (preferably before service is impacted).
- Persuading and explaining to all users that all incidents should be logged via the service desk. Awareness campaigns are particularly useful in this area.

# 27 PROBLEM MANAGEMENT

## INTRODUCTION AND SCOPE

Whereas incident management is concerned with the restoration of service, problem management is focused on the underlying cause. Problem management is responsible for the management of all IT problems. The process includes root cause analysis and arriving at the resolution of problems. Problem management remains responsible until resolutions are implemented via change management and release and deployment management.

Problem management provides value to an organisation by avoiding, reducing and mitigating the adverse business impact of problems. This allows services to be more available and to be more robust.

## PURPOSE AND OBJECTIVES

The objectives of problem management are:

- to prevent problems and resulting incidents from occurring;
- to stop repeat incidents happening;
- to mitigate and reduce the adverse impact of incidents that cannot be prevented.

Problem management, like most processes, has reactive and proactive aspects. From a reactive perspective, the purpose of the process is to manage the lifecycle of problems from identification to elimination by determining the root cause and then applying the necessary change(s) to prevent recurrence. From a proactive perspective, the purpose of the process is to prevent future incidents wherever possible or reduce the impact of those incidents that can't be prevented.

## BASIC CONCEPTS

An incident is the visible effect of something that has gone wrong. A problem is the underlying cause of one or more incidents.

### Problem models

A problem model is a similar idea to that of an incident model. Problem models provide a standardised approach to tackling problems.

## Difference between reactive and proactive

There are two aspects of problem management. Reactive problem management responds to incidents and problems that occur. The proactive side of problem management is concerned with preventing incidents and problems occuring. Proactive problem management is often triggered by continual service improvement.

A good analogy is to consider a Fire Service. Any Fire Service is going to be involved in fighting fires. This is the reactive part of their role. All Fire Services are also involved in fire prevention by raising public awareness and the installation and testing of smoke alarms and sensors. This is the proactive side. Problem management should have a similar split, ensuring that resources are involved in longer-term problem prevention as well as the here and now reactive response to problems and incidents. It is often difficult to release resources to the proactive side, especially when the reactive demands are high, but it is proactive problem prevention that allows organisations to become more mature in their service management.

## KEY ACTIVITIES

### The problem management process flow

The problem management process flow is illustrated in Figure 27.1 and contains the following steps:

- **Inputs to the process:** The inputs to problem management can come from a number of sources. These include incident management, event management and the service desk. Additionally, proactive problem management may identify problems. Suppliers and other processes such as release and deployment management, capacity management and availability management may also become aware of problems.

- **Problem detection:** Problems can be detected in many ways. The service desk may believe that one or more incidents are being caused by a particular problem. Second-line support areas may identify a problem when conducting incident handling. Problems can also be detected automatically by the service management tools in use. Proactive problem management will identify problems often before any incidents occur. Likewise, other processes such as release and deployment management and availability management will become aware of problems.

- **Problem logging:** It is crucial that the full details of the problem are recorded. This will allow analysis to take place and will enable comparisons to be made between problems. All incidents caused by the problem should be linked to the problem record allowing the scope and scale of the impact to be ascertained easily. The date and the time that all problems are logged should be recorded within the problem record.

- **Problem categorisation:** It is important to categorise problems and it is recommended that the same system is used as adopted by the incident management process for any particular organisation. Correct and meaningful categorisation will allow helpful metrics to be produced and enable proactive problem management to identify areas on which to concentrate.

## Figure 27.1  Problem management process flow

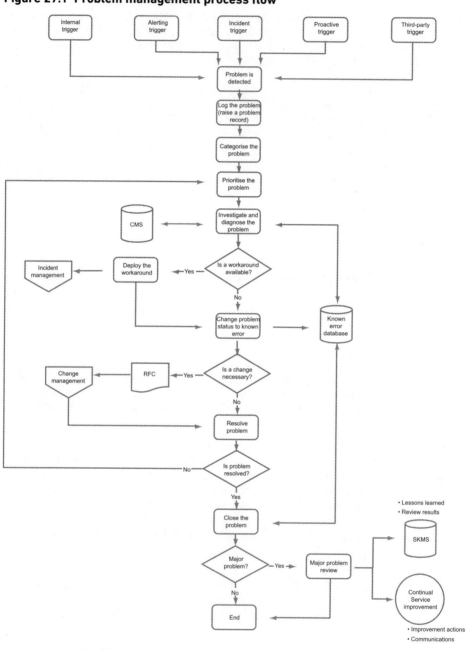

- **Problem prioritisation:** Problems should be prioritised in the same way as incidents. Table 27.1 shows a simplistic problem priority coding system.

**Table 27.1  A simplistic problem priority coding system**

|  |  | Impact | | |
| --- | --- | --- | --- | --- |
|  |  | High | Medium | Low |
|  | High | Priority 1 | Priority 2 | Priority 3 |
| **Urgency** | Medium | Priority 2 | Priority 3 | Priority 4 |
|  | Low | Priority 3 | Priority 4 | Priority 5 |

Target problem resolution times will have been allocated to each priority level. These will have been agreed with the business and recorded in the SLA.

One factor that will feed into the impact and urgency of problems is the rate of reoccurrence.

- **Problem investigation and diagnosis:** The aim of the investigation and diagnosis phase is to ascertain the root cause of the problem. The priority allocated to the problem should drive the number of resources working on the investigation and diagnosis. Priority should be reassessed during the lifetime of the problem to ensure that it remains correct.

There are various problem-solving techniques that can be employed to aid the diagnosis of problems. These include:

- **Kepner and Tregoe:** A logical approach to problem-solving starting with defining and then describing the problem. Possible causes are established and then probable causes tested and finally the true cause is verified.

- **Chronological analysis:** This approach sets out all the things that have happened in a timeline. This makes it clearer to see what has happened and allows focus on the critical part of the timeline.

- **Brainstorming:** Gathering together the key individuals involved with a problem in one place and mapping out all possible causes (and potential corrective activity). Such sessions should be under the control of the problem manager.

- **Pain value analysis:** This technique is useful for identifying which problems should be tackled in which order. Pain to a business can be defined in a number of different ways, for example the number of users impacted or potential financial loss. Pain value analysis provides a framework for deciding which problems are actually hurting the organisation most, allowing resources to be allocated where they are most needed.

- **Pareto analysis:** The Pareto principle is often referred to as the '80–20 rule'. The rule states that for many events, roughly 80 per cent of the effects come from only 20 per cent of the causes. This rule can be used in problem management to target those causes (problems) responsible for most of the incidents.

- **Workarounds:** Sometimes before permanent fixes can be found, workarounds are identified. This often takes place during the problem investigation and diagnosis phase. Workarounds are ways of restoring service that can be used without understanding the root cause. An obvious and frequently used example is the user who finds that their screen has 'frozen'. There could be any number of causes, but the first step, which quite often allows the user to carry on working while the root cause is determined, is usually to turn off the PC and then turn it back on again.

Problem records should remain open when a workaround has been identified and the workaround should be detailed in the problem record. Permanent fixes should still be progressed. However, there may be reasons why workarounds remain in place for some time. These reasons include:

- a permanent fix is too risky;

- a permanent fix is too costly;

- the business impact of the problem is not significant enough to justify further diagnosis at this time;

- the problem will be permanently fixed by a new release that is currently being planned.

- **Raising a known error record:** The known error database is an important source of information for the service desk and support groups handling incidents and problems. A known error record should be raised when the diagnosis has been completed and especially when a workaround has been identified.

A known error arises where there is a problem whose root cause has been identified and for which a workaround exists. They are usually created by problem management, although they may also be identified by suppliers or developers. They are managed through their lifecycle by problem management.

- **Problem resolution:** Once a permanent fix has been identified, it should be implemented as soon as possible. However, there may be good reasons for not doing this immediately. The reasons are similar to the reasons why organisations live with workarounds and include cost and risk. Additionally, an immediate fix may require a service outage which is not justifiable in the short term. A request for change (RFC) should be raised and progressed for any required change identified.

- **Problem closure:** Problem records should be closed once a change has successfully been applied. It is important that the problem record stays open until it is certain that the problem has been resolved. Checking that the problem has been resolved should be undertaken via testing. It may take some time to ensure that a fix has been successful, for example it may be the next time a particular process is used such as end of day, end of month, end of quarter, year-end or end of tax year.

- **Major problem review:** Whenever a major problem has occurred, a major problem review should be undertaken. Each organisation will have its own definition of a major problem based on the impact and urgency. It is crucial that these reviews look at lessons learnt rather than becoming 'allocation of blame' sessions. The output from a major problem review ought to include what went well, what went badly, what could be done better in the future, how could the problem have been prevented and how could the impact of the problem have been reduced.

## PROACTIVE PROBLEM MANAGEMENT

It is clearly better for any organisation to prevent incidents occurring rather than waiting for them to occur and then committing resource to fixing them, often repetitively over time. This is the basic principle of quality assurance, as opposed to quality control, and it is not only better for the business and its users but also more efficient for IT. Problem management is therefore one of the most important processes in helping reduce the amount of time IT staff spend 'fire fighting', particularly for second and third line teams whose primary role is project-related improvement work and for whom reacting to incidents is an unwanted interruption.

In operating proactively, problem management often works closely with both the availability management process and continual service improvement since each of these aspects has similar objectives, namely to protect the IT environment from disruption and improve services wherever it is cost-effective to do so.

Proactive activities can include analysing trends associated with historic incidents to identify and eliminate underlying infrastructure or application weaknesses. Proactive work may be initiated from a service improvement plan that has been created perhaps in response to poor performance or simply from a wish to improve performance, for instance in a competitive situation to gain an advantage over another service provider.

### EXAMPLE

An organisation realised that there would be huge issues and repercussions if they were to suffer a loss of personal or critical business data either through accident or hacking. They therefore decided to hold a 'pre-post' major incident review meeting and convened a major incident review to consider how they would respond should a breach occur in the future.

## RELATIONSHIPS WITH OTHER SERVICE MANAGEMENT PROCESSES

There are very close connections between problem management and incident management. Also, problem management needs to work closely with the service transition processes of change management, configuration management and release and deployment management.

Information about problems and known errors will come from processes such as availability management, capacity management and IT service continuity management. The proactive side of problem management has close relationships with both continual service improvement and availability management. Financial management and service level management provide some of the cost and service guidelines to which problem management adheres.

## METRICS

Metrics should be put in place to measure the effectiveness and the efficiency of the problem management process. Metrics should include:

- the percentage of problems resolved within the timescales set out in the SLA;
- the average cost of resolving a problem;
- the percentage of major problems where major problem reviews have been carried out;
- the percentage of actions from completed major problem reviews that have been completed;
- the number of known errors identified.

The actual number of problems identified during a period is useful to give an indication of the scale of issues and the resources required, but on its own it is not a measure of the effectiveness or efficiency of the process.

## ROLES

The key role is that of problem manager. The problem manager is responsible for problem management within the organisation. Larger organisations will have teams of problem managers. It is important that the problem manager can call on staff from a wide variety of support groups when tackling problems.

## CHALLENGES

Incident management focuses on restoring service as quickly as possible while problem management is concerned with ascertaining and removing the root cause of one or more incidents.

The two processes work closely together. However, there can at times be a tension between the incident management and problem management processes. Often the problem investigation and diagnosis phase can be time-consuming. If incident management has a quick workaround to restore service, they will want to use it. This may not aid problem management which needs to understand the root cause. Problem management may require an outage or to take a 'dump' of data which again may be at odds with incident management striving to get the service back running as soon as possible.

Other challenges include:

- ensuring that the incident and problem tools are compatible and communicate with each other;
- understanding the real business impact of problems.

# 28   IT OPERATIONS MANAGEMENT

## INTRODUCTION AND SCOPE

IT operations management is a function and not a process. It is responsible for operating the organisation's IT infrastructure and applications on a day-to-day basis. The IT infrastructure and applications underpin the organisation's services.

## PURPOSE AND OBJECTIVES

Delivery of stable service with unavailability minimised is the main objective.

IT operations management is the function that ensures that all the organisation's IT infrastructure and applications are managed and maintained on a day-to-day basis in order to deliver the agreed levels of service.

## KEY ACTIVITIES

IT operations management is made up of two parts:

- **Operations control:** Responsible for carrying out the day-to-day operational activities. This includes monitoring the IT infrastructure and applications and responding to events, incidents and problems. More specifically tasks include job scheduling, backup and restore, console management, print and output management as well as undertaking maintenance activities for technical management teams and application management teams.
- **Facilities management:** Responsible for the day-to-day management of the physical IT environment. This typically would include responsibility for the data centre, server rooms as well as recovery rooms and sites. The power supply and back-up power supply would also be in scope. If any part of the physical IT environment is outsourced, then the facilities management arm of IT operations management would be responsible for day-to-day management of the contract and the relationship with the supplier.

It is important that IT operations management is involved at the right time throughout the service management lifecycle and in the right way. More specifically:

- **Service strategy:** IT operations management will have an in-depth understanding of how current technology is used to deliver existing services. This understanding, together with an awareness of new and emerging technologies, allows IT operations management to have a meaningful input to the strategy phase of the service management lifecycle. It is crucial that those responsible for strategy use the knowledge that is available about how services are actually delivered on a day-to-day basis.

- **Service design:** Carrying out the activities set out in the service design phase is the responsibility of IT operations management. Therefore, it is important that IT operations management has the ability to input to this phase.

- **Service transition:** Testing is an area of service transition where you would expect IT operations management to be involved heavily. IT operations staff have the knowledge and understanding of the live environment, which allows them to ensure testing is correctly designed and executed. It may well be IT operations staff, under direction from service transition, who physically introduce releases to the live environment and monitor their progress.

- **Service operation:** This is the fundamental task of IT operations management. They maintain and monitor the components (infrastructure and applications) that underpin the services and react in a timely fashion to events, incidents and problems identified.

- **Continual service improvement:** Staff from IT operations management will always be looking for ways to improve the services and boost efficiency and effectiveness.

## RELATIONSHIPS WITH OTHER SERVICE MANAGEMENT FUNCTIONS

There may be overlaps between IT operations management and both technical management and application management. IT operations management is a distinct function but it is usual for teams from both application management and technical management to be part of this function.

Technical management is responsible for the IT infrastructure while application management is responsible for applications. Technical management has the same responsibilities for the IT infrastructure as application management has for applications.

# 29 EVENT MANAGEMENT

## INTRODUCTION AND SCOPE

Event management monitors all events throughout the organisation's IT infrastructure and applications to ensure normal operation. Event management handles normal messages as well as being there to detect, escalate and react to exceptions. It is a key activity of IT operations.

The event management process is responsible for managing events throughout their lifecycle.

Essentially an event represents any change of state that is important for managing services or configuration items. It is also used to denote an alert or notification raised by a monitoring tool or item. Alerts frequently require action by staff and may lead to incidents being raised, while notifications may simply be recorded.

Events can be split into three types:

- **Informational:** Such as notification of a scheduled job finishing or a user accessing an application.
- **Warning:** Including indications that utilisation of a particular CI has reached a certain percentage of capacity.
- **Exception:** Such as unauthorised software detected or failure of a component.

Event management can be used by any part of service management where there is a requirement to monitor and control an activity, as long as the monitoring and control can be automated. Event management requires the ability to raise automated alerts. If alerts cannot be raised, then only monitoring is taking place. Event management is more proactive than monitoring.

## PURPOSE AND OBJECTIVES

Event management is the service operation process responsible for ensuring that the infrastructure, applications and security that underpin IT services are proactively monitored with alerts being put in place and acted on.

## KEY ACTIVITIES

Event management follows a process similar to incident management (see Figure 29.1).

The stages of the process should ideally be automated within the selected tool(s), but manual intervention may be required at times.

The sooner events are detected, the sooner they can be tackled. For example, for a service that is required to be available from 7.00 a.m., it is desirable to have a number of alerts in place to indicate if any of the components required to provide that service are not available at a time prior to 7.00 a.m.

## RELATIONSHIPS WITH OTHER SERVICE MANAGEMENT PROCESSES

### Incident management

There is a close relationship between event management and incident management. The processes are similar and some events will be triggers for the incident management process. Proactive event management will reduce the number of incidents because action can be taken from warning events to prevent an incident.

### Other processes

Many areas of service management will identify areas that they want to control and monitor. Configuration management, availability management and capacity management will have a number of requirements for event management.

## Figure 29.1 The event management process

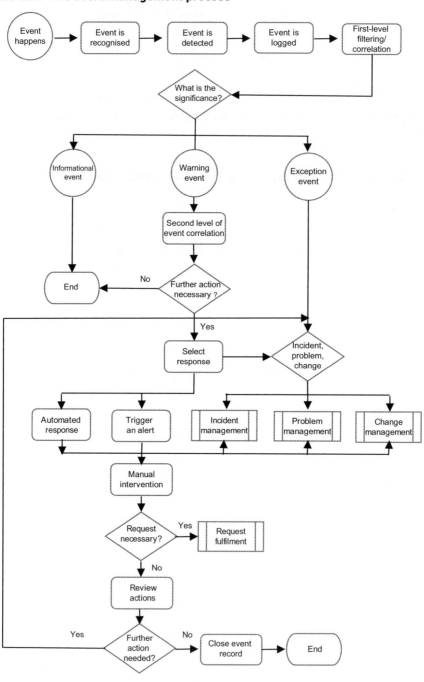

# 30 APPLICATION MANAGEMENT

## INTRODUCTION AND SCOPE

Application management is a function and not a process. It will manage applications through the totality of their lifecycle. This starts with the first business 'idea' and completes when the application is no longer required. Application management is involved in the design, testing and continual improvement of applications and the services that the applications support.

An application is any software program or programs that support a business process. Such applications, in conjunction with data, hardware, middleware and the operating system, make up the IT infrastructure that supports a service. It is not unusual for large organisations with a diverse set of services to have a high number of application teams. These teams may be grouped together depending on the type(s) of technology used in the applications that they support.

The applications may be developed in-house or they may be bought in. Bought-in applications will need varying degrees of customisation prior to release. For those teams responsible for bought-in applications, managing the ongoing relationship with the supplier (in conjunction with supplier management) is important.

Application management teams manage and support applications on a day-to-day basis. For example, they will usually be the functional escalation route used by the service desk when an incident or problem has been logged and categorised against their application.

## PURPOSE AND OBJECTIVES

Application management has two objectives:

- Custodian of technical knowledge and expertise relating to the managing of applications. Application management makes certain that the required technical knowledge to design, test, operate and continually improve applications is available.

- Provider of the actual resources to facilitate all phases of the service lifecycle, ensuring that staff are adequately trained and effective. It is often important for staff who are to be deployed in service operations to have been involved in the service design and the service transition activities for a particular application.

## RELATIONSHIP BETWEEN APPLICATION MANAGEMENT AND APPLICATION DEVELOPMENT

Application development teams are increasingly becoming accountable for the successful operation of applications they have designed. In parallel, the application management function is becoming more involved in application development. This has created a greater level of integration between the two functions but typically requires the following:

- A single interface to the business for requirements and specification setting.
- End-to-end accountability for applications from design to operation.
- A single change management process spanning development and operational environments.

## KEY ACTIVITIES

Application management has to be involved throughout the service management lifecycle. It is important that application management is involved at the right time and in the right way. More specifically:

- **Service strategy:** High-level requirements are the outputs of this phase. The decision-making criteria relating to whether applications are developed in-house or are bought in (and customised as necessary) are of particular relevance to applications management. Application management will have the knowledge and experience to contribute to this decision.

- **Service design:** How applications are to be designed and subsequently managed is established during the service design phase. Application management will have an understanding of how similar applications are presently managed and will provide information and views during the service design phase.

- **Service transition:** Application management will be included in testing and in ensuring that the testing process is appropriate and robust. Knowledge held within the application management teams on the applications and how they interface with each other and with the technical infrastructure will be used to help draw up test scripts. Known errors may be identified at this stage. The known errors may be eradicated or, after a cost and risk assessment, be allowed into the live environment with problem management and the known error database being updated.

- **Service operation:** Application management will typically be available to respond to support requests for the applications for which they are responsible. It is common for application management teams to undertake operational activities as part of the IT operations management function. Application management teams provide second-line support and are available for functional escalation relating to events, incidents and problems.

- **Continual service improvement:** The performance of applications which make up or underpin a service will be constantly monitored. Improvements will be identified and considered from the point of view of cost and urgency.

For applications that have been bought in, close liaison is required with the supplier to ensure that the organisation is aware of possible enhancements that may be considered for implementation.

## RELATIONSHIPS WITH OTHER SERVICE MANAGEMENT FUNCTIONS

### IT operations management, technical management

There may be overlaps between application management and both IT operations management and technical management. Application management is responsible for the applications while technical management is responsible for the IT infrastructure. Application management has the same responsibilities for the applications as technical management has for the IT infrastructure.

IT operations management is a distinct function, but it is usual for teams from both application management and technical management to be part of this function.

# 31 TECHNICAL MANAGEMENT

## INTRODUCTION AND SCOPE

Technical management is not a process, it is a function that provides the resources and ensures that knowledge of the relevant technologies is kept up to date.

How technical teams are managed will vary from organisation to organisation depending on scale and the blends of technologies used.

Technical management covers all the teams or areas that support the delivery and management of the IT infrastructure through the provision of technical knowledge and expertise. This includes teams such as networks, mainframe, middleware, desktop, server and database.

## PURPOSE AND OBJECTIVES

Technical management has two objectives:

- Custodian of technical knowledge and expertise relating to the IT infrastructure of the organisation. Technical management makes certain that the required technical knowledge to design, test, operate and continually improve IT services is available.

- Provider of the actual resources to facilitate all phases of the service lifecycle, ensuring that staff are adequately trained and effective. It is often important for staff who are to be deployed in service operations to have been involved in the service design and the service transition activities for a particular service.

## KEY ACTIVITIES

Technical management has to be involved throughout the service management lifecycle. It is important that technical management is involved at the right time and in the right way. More specifically:

- **Service strategy:** The knowledge and expertise required to manage and operate the IT infrastructure will be identified in the service strategy phase of the service management lifecycle. Technical management teams will have an important input to the agreement on standards for technical architecture.

- **Service design:** During the service design phase, technical management teams will provide expertise on the IT infrastructure and will make suggestions for how new parts of the infrastructure can be managed at an operational level.

- **Service transition:** Technical management will be included in testing and in ensuring that the testing process is appropriate and robust. The knowledge held within the technical management teams of the technical infrastructure and how it interfaces with the applications will be used to help draw up test scripts.

- **Service operation:** It is common for technical management teams to undertake operational activities as part of the IT operations management function. Technical management teams provide second-line support and are available for functional escalation relating to events, incidents and problems.

- **Continual service improvement:** The performance of the IT infrastructure components that underpin a service will be constantly monitored. Improvements will be identified and considered from the point of view of cost and urgency. For IT infrastructure that has been bought in, close liaison is required with the supplier to ensure that the organisation is aware of possible enhancements and that these are considered for implementation.

## RELATIONSHIPS WITH OTHER SERVICE MANAGEMENT FUNCTIONS

### IT operations management, application management

There may be overlaps between technical management and both IT operations management and application management. Technical management is responsible for the IT infrastructure while application management is responsible for applications. Technical management has the same responsibilities for the IT infrastructure as application management has for applications.

IT operations management is a distinct function but it is usual for teams from both application management and technical management to be part of this function.

# 32 THE SEVEN-STEP IMPROVEMENT PROCESS

## INTRODUCTION AND SCOPE

The seven-step improvement process is the sole process within the continual service improvement part of the lifecycle. However, it offers a repeatable and effective way to identify and apply improvement to any aspect of service provision in any part of the service lifecycle. It is based on the 'Plan–Do–Check–Act' cycle of improvement proposed by W. Edwards Deming and also shows how the cycle fits into the data-to-information-to-knowledge-to-wisdom structure of knowledge management.

## PURPOSE AND OBJECTIVES

The purpose of the seven-step improvement process is to undertake consistently and efficiently a cycle of improvement based on defining the steps needed to identify, define, gather, process, analyse, present and implement improvements as the basic building blocks of continual service improvement.

The objectives of the seven-step improvement process are to:

- define a set of measures that are relevant to business requirements and which will support the identification of effective improvement opportunities;
- adopt a structured approach to gathering, processing and analysing the measurement data in order to identify improvement opportunities;
- communicate those improvement opportunities so that appropriate decisions can be taken about actions.

The seven-step improvement process is fundamental in supporting CSI and operates across the entire service lifecycle. It focuses on identifying improvement opportunities, not only for the processes and services, but also for the disciplines implemented as part of each of the lifecycle stages, including the discipline of CSI itself.

Value is created by ensuring that the services and the mechanisms for delivering those services continue to align with and meet business requirements and by identifying opportunities for continual improvement.

## ACTIVITIES, METHODS AND TECHNIQUES

Table 32.1 expands on the individual steps. Note that it is a closed loop, feeding back into strategic decision making. As such it is easy to draw a parallel with the Deming Plan–Do–Check–Act cycle.

**Figure 32.1 The seven-step improvement process**

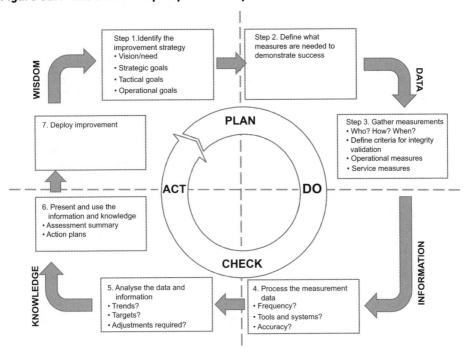

## ROLES

Everybody within the organisation has a role to play in continual improvement. The key role that is essential to the effective implementation of this process is the CSI manager.

This is role of real responsibility and either needs to have the appropriate seniority and authority or have clear and unambiguous senior support. Responsibilities include:

- developing the CSI domain;

- communicating the vision of CSI across the organisation;

- working with the service owners and service level manager to define the monitoring requirements, identify and prioritise improvement opportunities and establish service improvement plans (SIPs);

- identifying frameworks, models and standards that will support CSI activities;
- ensuring that activities are coordinated throughout the entire service lifecycle;
- presenting improvement recommendations to senior management.

There is also likely to be an analyst who will be responsible for gathering and manipulating data, and presenting it in the desired formats.

**Table 32.1  The seven-step improvement process**

| | | |
|---|---|---|
| Step 1 | Identify the improvement strategy | Take into account vision, strategy, goals and objectives to determine what to measure. These measurements should enable the provider to demonstrate value to the business by linking back through to key business drivers. |
| Step 2 | Define what measures are needed | There may be a gap between the capabilities of current tools and mechanisms to provide the necessary information. If the desired data really cannot be gathered or if the cost is prohibitive, the measures in Step 1 may need to be revisited. |
| Step 3 | Gather measurements | Use monitoring to gather the data. Monitoring may be either automatic or manual. Extra care needs to be taken to ensure that manually gathered data is accurate and consistent. |
| Step 4 | Process the measurement data | Convert the data gathered into the required format for the audience. This can be seen as turning data into information. |
| Step 5 | Analyse the data and information | Transform the information into knowledge. Develop an understanding of the real meaning of identified patterns and trends, by querying the results to understand its intrinsic value. |
| Step 6 | Present and use the information and knowledge | Communicate the information at the right level of detail for the audience and in a format that is understandable, provides value and will support informed decision making. |
| Step 7 | Deploy improvement | Use the wisdom gained to make the necessary changes throughout the lifecycle. |

# SECTION 4:
# MEASUREMENT, METRICS AND THE DEMING CYCLE

# 33 MEASUREMENT AND METRICS

## INTRODUCTION

While measurement and metrics are neither processes nor functions, this chapter earns its place here because it is difficult to overestimate their importance.

Measurement is a prerequisite to improvement. Put simply, if you can't measure something, you can't improve it or show that it has improved. The reason for this is that to make an improvement, you have to identify that something has gone wrong or not happened and then understand why. Only then can you diagnose the root cause and apply a change to eliminate it, preventing the same thing from happening again and thereby improving performance.

There are other reasons for measurement:

- To demonstrate that an operation or service has performed according to requirements or specification. An example of this would be the publication of a train company's performance against its service levels for the timetable (i.e. the percentage of trains that arrived on time).

- To prove to a stakeholder that they received what they commissioned and for which they might have paid (e.g. an independent audit of the performance of a third-party sales company engaged to generate new sales from a call centre).

- To compare the performance of one operation or service against another, as in a benchmark.

- To establish a baseline that represents the present situation and from which to demonstrate a variation in the future (e.g. the share price of a new company on the day it goes public and trading in shares starts is a baseline).

These examples show that measurements are justified for reasons other than improvement. However, only when used to create improvement can they tangibly increase value for an organisation and its customers. It is for this reason that measurements and metrics as a topic is included within the continual service improvement part of the service lifecycle.

## KEY PERFORMANCE INDICATORS AND METRICS

There is often confusion concerning the differences between key performance indicators (KPIs) and metrics.

In essence, all KPIs are metrics, but not all metrics are KPIs.

To expand slightly on this, the following view of KPIs is helpful: 'metrics are used to help an organisation define and evaluate how successful it is, typically in terms of making progress towards its long-term organisational goals.'

In summary therefore, a KPI is simply a more important metric because it references goals rather than just performance. As such, there are typically fewer KPIs than metrics and we often find that KPIs are expressed in terms of two or more metrics. For example, 'number of incidents reported' and 'number of incidents resolved by the service desk' are both metrics, but 'percentage of incidents resolved by the service desk' expresses the latter as a proportion of the former to produce a meaningful measure of quality or KPI for a customer.

### Three types of metric

In support of continual service improvement, there are three distinct types of metric:

- **Technology metrics:** These metrics are associated with components such as 'mean time between failures'. Usually these metrics are used internally to understand the capability of the technology components on which a service depends to remain in service.

- **Process metrics:** These are typically used to measure the quality, performance, value and compliance of a service management process as a way of identifying improvement opportunities. An example is 'percentage of failed changes'. These metrics are used to ensure that the processes are conforming to documented procedures.

- **Service metrics:** These are used to measure and report on an end-to-end service, for example 'percentage availability of the web service in the last month'. These are the metrics that are used in performance reports provided to customers.

In summary, measurements and metrics are focused on the key attributes of performance, compliance, quality and value.

### Baselines

Baselines have two purposes:

- To provide a reference point against which to demonstrate future improvement.
- To measure the health of an operation or process to see if it requires attention.

Baselines can and should be established at strategic, tactical and operation levels. Initially, baseline measures may be difficult to compile and of questionable accuracy. However, the data is still valuable as a focus for improvement potential.

## Critical success factors

Critical success factors (CSFs) identify areas that are critical to the success of the enterprise and, as such, they tend to be high level and few in number. For example, the involvement of the business could be a CSF for IT service. CSI might have senior management involvement or commitment as a CSF. Improved IT service quality could be a sensible CSF for IT service management. We might see clearly defined roles and responsibilities as a CSF in any organisation.

For CSFs to be more than just a vague concept there has to be some way of measuring them: a way of calibrating our performance against the things that are most important to our business; that define our success or failure. To achieve this we need to break down each CSF into things that we can measure and that will help us assess how well we are doing. We need something we can measure that will give us a characteristic or a numerical value that will tell us whether our goals are being achieved.

Earlier, we described key performance indicators (KPIs) as important because they reference goals rather than just performance. This discussion of CSFs shows how organisational goals, critical success factors, KPIs and metrics are interrelated in our performance management and improvement framework.

Baselines tell us where we started from, or where we were the last time we checked, whereas goals, CSFs and KPIs tell us where we are going and if we have arrived, or at least if we are still going in the right direction.

## USING METRICS AND KPIS TO IMPROVE PERFORMANCE

It is not the aim of this book to provide formal guidance on the use of measurement in IT service management. Many books have been written on the subject and a foundation level syllabus will not require the candidate to achieve such expertise. However, some guidance on constructing meaningful measures and reports is useful in order to help you establish a measurement framework that you can use for performance improvement and in which you have confidence in its integrity and value.

Measures should always encourage the correct behaviour. Measures that give incentive to productivity without a corresponding quality measure usually don't do this.

### EXAMPLE

Having a target for 'number of calls handled per service desk analyst per day' will only encourage analysts to shorten calls, typically to the detriment of the caller. In a real-life example, one member of a sales team promoting a new product consistently sold more products than her colleagues. However, when management monitored the calls to understand the secret of her success, they were horrified to hear that she was promising full refunds if the buyer was in any way unhappy. She achieved the highest sales but also created the highest refund levels, except she wasn't measured against refunds!

Measures should be meaningful to those receiving the performance reports. It may be easy for IT to report 'mean time between service incidents' or perhaps 'percentage availability of service X', but the service recipient may only be interested in or understand the number and duration of outages and, more importantly, what the service provider is doing to prevent future outages.

Measures should be unambiguous. For example, service desks are increasingly recognising the importance of using 'first-line resolution rate' as a KPI. This is entirely appropriate, provided it is properly measured. However, there are significant variations in the way this KPI is measured that make it very hard to compare across organisations or establish a target value. Most organisations measure first-line resolution rate by dividing the total number of logged calls by the number of logged calls resolved by the service desk without escalation, expressed as a percentage. The simplest reason for variations is because contacts to the service desk can be broadly divided into incidents, service requests (including password resets) and information requests. Incidents are much harder to fix at first line than either of the others. Therefore by failing to separate out the incidents from the requests, the first-line resolution rate will vary according to the mix of contact types as well as the performance of the service desk, making the measure meaningless.

A further distortion of measurement occurs with variations against the period over which a measure is taken. Put simply, the longer the period, the easier it is to meet the target. For example, if the target availability of a service is expressed as 99 per cent, it is easier to meet this over a monthly period than a weekly or daily period. Either is valid, but each organisation needs to decide which is most applicable.

## METRICS IN REPORTS

Focus on the exceptions. Where you are reporting measures internally, rather than to a customer, report the exceptions rather than the conformance. For example, if 200 changes were implemented last month and four failed, instead of reporting a 98 per cent success rate and patting each other on the back, report that there were four failures. These represent the improvement opportunity and provide a focus for action.

KPIs and metrics should therefore be constructed in a way that all report recipients understand and accept as an accurate measure of performance. When comparing or benchmarking such measures, ensure that the values against which you compare are constructed on the same basis: they often aren't!

When constructing performance reports do not rely solely on charts or numeric tables but use both together for a full picture. Charts are useful for showing trends and exceptions but are often manipulated to create a specific perception, for example by starting the y-axis at a value other than zero to increase apparent variations, or by excluding exceptions to better define a pattern. Numbers show absolute values and generally have higher integrity, but are less useful for showing trends.

Most recipients of reports focus on exceptions, so where there is an exception, it is the responsibility of the report creator to explain the cause. Where the exception is undesirable, the explanation should include the actions taken to prevent future exceptions. The combination of charts, numbers and explanations in a report will always provide more value than a report missing any one of these.

# 34  THE DEMING CYCLE

## INTRODUCTION

Many organisations attempt service improvement through 'big bang' implementations and by the utilisation of large projects. This may be appropriate, but often small iterative step improvements to a service or process can be more efficient and less risky.

The Deming Cycle was introduced by W. Edwards Deming as a method for quality improvement. If processes are in place, they can be measured. Changes can be made to those process and the impact of the changes assessed via further measurement. This enables ongoing measurable improvement.

---

**Figure 34.1  The Deming Cycle**

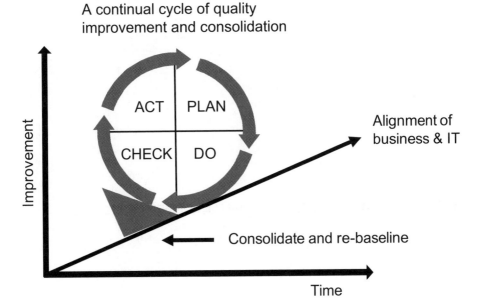

A continual cycle of quality improvement and consolidation

Improvement

ACT    PLAN

CHECK    DO

Alignment of business & IT

Consolidate and re-baseline

Time

Over time, the step improvements enable the service or process to become more mature. After each phase of Plan–Do–Check–Act, there is a period of consolidation to enable new improvements to 'bed-in' and to ensure that they are doing what they were intended to do.

## PURPOSE AND OBJECTIVES

The objective is continual service improvement. This relates to the services provided by the organisation and also to the processes used to deliver those services. The Deming Cycle may be used to improve, for example, an online ordering service or the service level management process within an organisation.

## KEY ACTIVITIES

The integration of the Plan–Do–Check–Act cycle with the seven-step improvement process identifies the activities of each stage as follows:

### Plan

1. Identify the strategy for improvement.
2. Define what you will measure.

### Do

3. Gather the data.
4. Process the data.

### Check

5. Analyse the information and data.
6. Present and use the information.

### Act

7. Implement improvement.

## RELATIONSHIPS WITH OTHER SERVICE MANAGEMENT PROCESSES

The Deming Cycle can be used in order to improve any of the service management processes.

# APPENDIX
# EXAM TECHNIQUES

## INTRODUCTION

Sitting any sort of test or exam is stressful, but candidates should remember that a foundation level exam is usually testing their basic understanding of the subject and terminology. For many it is a stepping-stone to more advanced training and qualifications and is therefore designed to be passable by the vast majority of candidates.

There are a number of techniques and hints to keep in mind when sitting a foundation level exam. Using these techniques and hints should enable candidates to maximise their scores. There is, of course, no substitute for a having a good knowledge of the topics included in the syllabus.

## EXAM TECHNIQUES

Before taking the exam, make sure that you are as prepared and relaxed as possible: visit the facilities, have a drink, try to get comfortable. When you start the exam adopt a methodical approach to ensure that you don't miss questions and, if time permits, check your answers.

- If there are 40 questions and the time allowed is 60 minutes, you have about 90 seconds for each. This doesn't sound like much time, but it is. In reality, many questions will take you much less time than this.

- Read each question carefully, paying particular attention to negatives, such as 'which of the following is NOT true?'. Many questions are phrased in this way simply because it is easier for the question setters to think up one wrong example than three. Also, pay attention to questions that are phrased, 'which of the following is the BEST answer?'. This indicates that all four answers potentially have some merit.

- Always work on eliminating the wrong answers first. This will help to avoid making simple mistakes and can leave you with perhaps two options instead of four and a better chance of selecting the correct answer.

- Answer the straightforward questions first and return to more complex ones, or ones that you are unsure of, later.

- If you think you have found an obvious right answer, sense-check that all the other options are wrong.

- Answer all the questions. Don't leave blanks on the answer grid.

- When tackling questions that you are unsure of, try the following:

  - Try to eliminate some of the options.

  - See if there are any clues in another question.

  - In the final resort, take an educated guess.

- Take care in changing an answer. Unless it is clearly wrong (e.g. because you misread the question initially) your first instinct is often proven right.

Points to remember:

- There is no negative marking (i.e. marks are not deducted for wrong answers).

- There aren't any trick questions; the objective is to test your knowledge and understanding.

# INDEX